Design in the 20th Century

Nationalism and Internationalism

Jeremy Aynsley

Victoria & Albert Museum

Acknowledgements

I would like to thank the Victoria and Albert Museum for the opportunity to work on the new display of the 20th Century Gallery. During the preparation of this Gallery, I learnt a great deal from the curatorial staff of the Museum. Especially, I shared discussion with members of the Project Team, Kevin Edge, Brian Griggs, Margaret Knight and Susan Lambert on the plausibility of taking a thematic approach to the history of design in the twentieth century.

There are many other Museum staff who have helped towards this publication with their generous exchange of ideas; in particular Stephen Astley, Neil Harvey, Eva White and Christopher Wilk contributed expertise from their respective Collections. Additionally I would like to acknowledge the support of the staff of the National Art Library. My thanks also go to Emily King, who provided excellent assistance with the picture research, to Richard Davis for his photography and to my editor, John Taylor.

Finally, I would like to thank members of the Research Department: Charles Saumarez Smith and Katrina Royall for their consistent interest in this project; the students on the MA in History of Design, run jointly by the Royal College of Art, London and the Victoria and Albert Museum, for providing a stimulating environment in which to develop ideas; and fellow teaching staff, Gillian Naylor, Penny Sparke and John Styles for their encouragement.

First published by the Victoria & Albert Museum 1993
© The Trustees of the Victoria & Albert Museum

British Library Cataloguing-in-Publication Data
A catalogue record for this book is available from the British Library

ISBN 1 85177 121 2

Designed by Karen Wilks

Printed in England by BAS Printers

Contents

Introduction

Terminology

Like all significant terms, 'internationalism' and 'nationalism' and their derivatives are historically constructed and have meanings which change over time. When applied to the decorative arts and design they may become more historically specific, but their meaning is equally fluid.

It is perhaps useful to start by exploring some of the characteristics of this fluidity. The sort of questions to ask include:

1) How can the form, material and technique of a piece of design embody national or international concerns?

2) Can there be national traditions in the systems of manufacture? How does a consciously international designer or company approach the organisation of their practice?

3) Are the categories mutually exclusive, or can the same object contain both a national and international aspect?

Many of the circumstances which determine whether a design is considered national or international lie beyond the individual object, in the structures which help it to be bought or to be used by different groups. For example, the twentieth century has witnessed a professionalisation of most areas of design activity. Selections are made by official government bodies and professional groups, who review the health of their design, and award prizes, adding value and sometimes moulding taste in so doing. In turn, many politicians and political agencies have questioned how national traditions or a sense of history can be evoked in an object of everyday life: a car, an advertisement or an item of clothing (Fig. 1).

The most obvious examples of consciously controlled national traditions in our century are found under totalitarian political systems, when direct government control has been imposed.[1] However, all nations address the question of the identity of their industries and develop complex forms of marketing and propaganda

© 1965 VOLKSWAGEN OF AMERICA, INC.

Think small.

Our little car isn't so much of a novelty any more.

A couple of dozen college kids don't try to squeeze inside it.

The guy at the gas station doesn't ask where the gas goes.

Nobody even stares at our shape.

In fact, some people who drive our little flivver don't even think 32 miles to the gallon is going any great guns.

Or using five pints of oil instead of five quarts.

Or never needing anti-freeze.

Or racking up 40,000 miles on a set of tires.

That's because once you get used to some of our economies, you don't even think about them any more.

Except when you squeeze into a small parking spot. Or renew your small insurance. Or pay a small repair bill. Or trade in your old VW for a new one.

Think it over.

to project this identity systematically in the international arena. At a more subliminal level, postage stamps, currency, a nation's flags and the uniforms of officials often provide foreign observers with their first and lasting impressions of national character (Fig. 2).

As early as the Middle Ages, before any nation states had properly emerged, cultural activities crossed national, linguistic and social boundaries. During the late eighteenth and nineteenth centuries national consciousness developed, nation states were consolidated and political nationalism emerged. In reaction against this political nationalism and the wars fought on its behalf, the twentieth century has witnessed renewed interest in internationalism, especially since the First World War. In recent years it may have become more appropriate to think in terms of regional-global distinctions, rather than nationalism or internationalism, for reasons which will be made clear below.

1. 'Think Small'. Advertisement by Doyle, Dane and Bernbach, 1962

A German product is recast by an American 'invention', the clever copyline of conceptual advertising. The campaign by Doyle, Dane and Bernbach won many awards for its novel approach to car promotion. At a time of an appeal to conspicuous consumption in car marketing it stressed the Volkswagen Beetle's other, idiosyncratic qualities.

2. *The Book of Road Signs*, by Dudley Noble, printed by William Clowes, for the British Road Federation Ltd, London 1946

First recognition of a country's national identity is often through road signs. The commentary in this book pointed out that signage instilled identity across a colonial Empire at that time, thereby also working ideologically.

SWEDEN

BULGARIA

YUGO-SLAVIA

HOLLAND

3. Simon Benninck (1483-1561) 'Leaf from a Kalendar of a Book of Hours, the Month of September' Watercolour E. 4576 – 1910

Visual culture can acquire meaning independently of linguistic or political boundaries. During the late fifteenth century, although different areas of Northern Europe and Spain still produced distinctive regional styles, art and design developed with common characteristics of ornament, architectural forms and highly worked detail.

Internationalism

Broad tendencies

'The international character of modern decorative art was an outgrowth of industrial society as a whole rather than of narrower national cultures.' Julius Meier Graefe (1867-1935)[2]

Before the evolution of nation states, art and design styles were created and understood internationally. Byzantine style, the Romanesque and the Gothic knew no frontiers. The possession of 'style' was the privilege of ruling groups, especially the princes of state and church. In late fifteenth-century Europe, via trade routes between Venice, northern France, Flanders and the northern Rhine, a kind of art developed which depended on highly stylised decorative detail for its effect (Fig. 3). It has since become known as 'The International Gothic' or 'The International Style'.[3] Transcending regional barriers of language, it worked as a visual language across political frontiers, alongside well-developed conventions of trade and a language for commercial transactions. Crucially, it indicated how taste and cultural values were transferable, crossing national boundaries to work in different contexts.

When dealing with designed objects and their makers, it is useful initially to distinguish between an implicit and an intended international character. Often international character is embraced passively rather than consciously: more important is the way in which internationalism is used to represent a coherent set of beliefs. This is often informed by political opinion and philosophical principles. Internationalism of this kind can be identified as a central characteristic of the Enlightenment.[4] It was first advocated by progressives, who saw the future as one of co-operation across national boundaries in matters of legal rights and political enfranchisement. To Jeremy Bentham (1748-1832), the British humanist philosopher, for example, the term was new when applied to the legal system in 1780: 'It is calculated to express, in a more significant way, the branch of law which goes commonly under the "law of nations".'[5]

4. A page from the catalogue for the General Electric Co., 1911-12

GEC, originally an American firm, was one of the first multi-national electrical companies. This page announced a range of electric kettles from the 'Archer' system. Its catalogue was 'of everything electrical'; goods from the catalogue were available to retailers throughout the world.

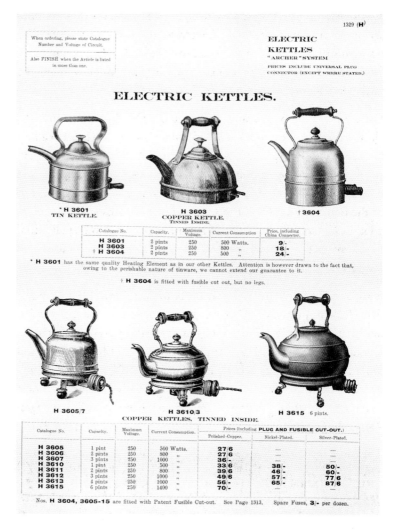

The concept 'internationalism' is often used to denote varied types of systems agreed between nation states. In reaction to laissez-faire trade and the growth of competition in the nineteenth century, commercial practices were reformed. Consequently such matters as maritime law, weights and measurement, time, and eventually power-sources were all standardised on an international basis. These reforms carried important implications for design as they provided the basic terminology by which design could be communicated. For instance, units to measure electricity were standardised in the

1890s, allowing multi-national companies to develop (Fig. 4). As a writer in the magazine *The Electrician* announced in 1893: 'To distinguish these units as now defined from the definitions given by previous meetings or congresses, they are denominated the international ohm, the international ampere.'[6]

Once units of power supply were standardised, it followed that electrical companies could diversify and plan international markets for electrical equipment. Another crucial development which enabled design to operate internationally was the system of patent and copyright laws. Copyright arrangements, for example, were agreed by the Berne Convention of 1886. This protected artists' and designers' published ideas and defined their sphere of influence and application. Similarly, patents were used to protect design innovations and product originality in an increasingly international context.

Early attempts to work internationally often followed the principle that characteristics from diverse cultural origins could be distilled into a simpler version. Esperanto is an interesting example. Attempts to find an international language were prompted by the technical innovation of telegraphic agencies in the 1870s. Esperanto was developed as a 'universal' language, with its basis in Latin, by Louis Zamenhof in 1887. Taking characteristics from several languages, Zamenhof combined these to find more general underlying

5. Lettering from Trajan's Column, from a plaster cast in the Victoria and Albert Museum, London The Cast Courts opened in 1873 Sculpture Department 1864-128

An inscription was cut in stone on the base of the Trajan Column in Rome, AD 113, to commemorate the successful campaigns by the Emperor against the Dacians of the Danube frontier. The seriffed Roman alphabet used here has formed the basis of alphabets in the Western world with surprisingly little variation ever since.

principles. Although not taken up widely, it reflected inter-nationalist aspirations and proved instructive to designers in applying a synthetic approach.

A closer look at design for the written word clarifies this. In many ways the carved, handwritten and printed alphabet has always been an adaptable design with a common use in spite of differences in language and nationality (Fig. 5). The Roman alphabet has been used extensively in the Western world since the Holy Roman Empire. Although each generation of users has contributed revisions, the ingredients of letter forms and their proportions have remained remarkably consistent. The possibilities for adaptation increased with the invention of movable type in the fifteenth century, when regional printers produced versions which broke with convention. As a result 'schools' or national styles of printing evolved.[7] Perhaps the need for analytical thinking required of the typographer has encouraged a tendency for international communication to feature as a priority in printed design (Fig. 6).

A step towards standardisation of type-size was made under Louis XIV and the French Court at the Imprimerie Royale in Paris in 1716, when the standard height of a letter became '10.5 lines'.[8] In the nineteenth century French and American standard units of measurement for type bodies, the point size, allowed for compatibility between typefaces and between individual printers in different countries. Paper, inks and typefaces all underwent mechanisation, while upon its invention photography came to be regarded as the naturally 'international' medium of visual communication. Increasingly, instructions in many areas of design could be given in one country, for manufacture to be carried out in another (Fig. 7).

In the early twentieth century, a general desire to cross frontiers of communication led to studies of signs and symbols. Cognitive and behavioural psychology were applied to the understanding of human motives in terms of perception (Fig. 8).[9] Poster artists, followed by advertising agencies, developed ways in which word and image could be combined to communicate across national boundaries, recognising the financial benefits of campaigns if used

ERS LIGHT CONDENSED 686, 48 Didot
ERS MEDIUM CONDENSED 690, 48 Didot

REGD. TRADE MARK
MONOTYPE

E MARK – UNIVERS

CDEFGHIJKLMNOPQRSTUVWXYZ&

4567890 .,:;!?"-([—

defghijklmnopqrstuvwxyz

ERS EXTRA BOLD EXPANDED 695, 28 Didot
ERS ULTRA BOLD EXPANDED 697, 28 Didot

REGD. TRADE MARK
MONOTYPE

MARK – UNIVERS

CDEFGHIJKLMNOPQRSTUVW

Z& 1234567890 .,:;!?"-([—

:defghijklmnopqrstuvwxyz

ERS MEDIUM 689, 48 Didot

REGD. TRADE MARK
MONOTYPE

E MARK – UNIVERS

CDEFGHIJKLMNOPQRST

WXYZ&.,:;!?"-([—

cdefghijklmnopqrstuvwxyz

CDEFGHIJKLMNOPQRST

WXYZ&.,:;!?"-([

cdefghijklmnopqrstuvwxyz

34567890

34567890

The creation of Univers marked an important milestone in the history of type design. For the first time a complete type family had been planned in advance, and each of the 20 variants was worked out in detail before the first matrix was struck. Adrian Frutiger started work on the design in 1952, and the first 'Monotype' matrices were made available in 1961. Like many typographers, Frutiger felt dissatisfied with the wide variety of sanserif faces at his disposal. It was his idea to create a new design which would meet contemporary needs by providing for greater variations of weight and width, whilst at the same time integrating the family in all its different aspects. Univers is being cut by The Monotype Corporation in collaboration with Deberny & Peignot, who originated it, and it has been designed for filmsetting as well as for hand and machine composition.

SIONS FOR ALL DISPLAY SIZES AVAILABLE ARE SHOWN BELOW

6. Three display cards for 'Univers', a typeface designed by Adrian Frutiger (Swiss, b.1928) produced by The Monotype Corporation, about 1956

One of many designs to have claimed a 'universal' intention in its title, Univers became accepted as a functional typeface on a worldwide scale. Conceived in Zurich in 1949, it was designed for the Deberny-Peignot type-foundry in Paris in 1954-57 as a family of typefaces of different sizes and weights.

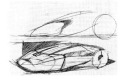

7. Copy of a sketch for the Venus project, 1989 International Automotive Design Studio, USA Telefax copy of a drawing in felt-tip pen E. 165 – 1992

In the early stages of a project, members of a design team need not necessarily work together in the same place. As this fax copy shows they do not even have to be in the same country. At the start of the Venus project the Worthing studio in Britain and the IAD studio in California were both contributing.

8. International picture language: the first rules of 'Isotype' by Otto Neurath (Austrian, 1882-1945), published by Basic English Publishing, 1936 L. 3923 – 1968

The 'isotype' (International System of Typographic Picture Education) developed by Neurath in Vienna was intended as a simplified visual language to convey statistical information and represents an early example of information design aimed at international use.

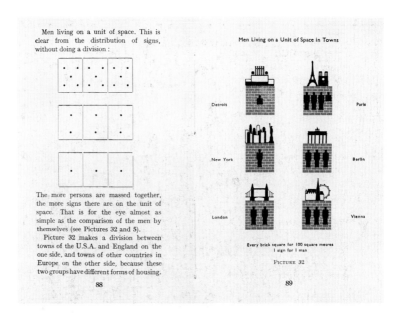

Men living on a unit of space. This is clear from the distribution of signs, without doing a division :

The more persons are massed together, the more signs there are on the unit of space. That is for the eye almost as simple as the comparison of the men by themselves (see Pictures 32 and 5).
Picture 32 makes a division between towns of the U.S.A. and England on the one side, and towns of other countries in Europe on the other side, because these two groups have different forms of housing.

88

Men Living on a Unit of Space in Towns

Detroit   Paris

New York   Berlin

London   Vienna

Every brick square for 100 square metres
I sign for I man

PICTURE 32

89

in many countries without substantial changes in language (Fig. 9).[10] Whereas some products need to be aimed at a national, even regional public, campaigns for others are stridently international in both visual language and copyline (Fig. 10).

The way in which design participates in the political and economic structure of a nation has been the subject of much theoretical writing. For a long time such participation has been considered benign, symptomatic of a modern, liberal, scientifically-based social force. With the demise in the certain faith in modernity and Modernism in the mid–twentieth century one crucial underlying question which remains concerns the way culture reflects the political attitudes of a country. Can design resist straightforward alliances with a political regime to construct its own autonomous identity? Most commentators agree with the view that design, like other cultural manifestations, has a relative autonomy. It is sufficiently independent to define its own languages, but nonetheless represents broad tendencies within a political economy. Antoni Gramsci (1891-1937) addressed such issues as someone interested in Marxist political revolution. He developed the concept of 'hegemony' to describe the dominance of the values of one class or nation over

9. Poster advertising 'Cirio foodstuffs', by Leonetto Cappiello (Italian, 1875-1924) c. 1923 Colour lithograph, 140 x 100.3 cm E86 – 1973

From the beginning of the century poster artists developed solutions to designs which were flexible. In this case the product range is announced without the presence of any linguistic barrier. Instead, a manufacturer's identity is reinforced by products aimed at consumers in many countries.

10. 'Nike' Air Max running shoe, designed by Nike, California, USA, made in Korea, 1992

In certain fashionable items the distinction between trademark, advertisement and object is collapsed. The word 'Nike' and the shape of the shoe work as international signifiers of status regardless of the shoe's context. The firm, Nike, takes its name from the winged goddess of Victory.

others.[11] Gramsci argued that such values were not expressed in political organisations alone, but also in the intellectual and material cultures of a nation. Such an idea may be useful when thinking about the implications of increasing internationalism in the twentieth century. Gramsci's notion of hegemony offers one way of considering the spread of product design and consumer goods and the homogenisation of life in a technologically advanced world (Fig. 11).

11. Election Poster 'Deutschland Is It?' for the Aktionsbündnis Vereinigte Linke (Action Alliance United Left) East Germany, 1990, designed by Mahlke Screenprint in red, 43.1 x 59.1 cm E. 2083 – 1990

Produced for the East German elections of 18 March 1990 following the fall of the Berlin Wall, the design of this poster is based on a famous advertising campaign for the internationally recognised soft drink company Coca-Cola. It simultaneously draws attention to the cultural dominance of the American lifestyle and the political choice of unification facing voters.

This becomes an acute point of debate whenever political regimes change. In the contemporary world, designers from developing or post-colonial countries question how to integrate indigenous craft traditions and whether to 'westernise' totally.[12] Meanwhile architects, artists and designers in countries of the former Soviet bloc consider which aspects of the regime prior to 1989 to maintain, which national traditions from before the Second World War to revive, and which contemporary values to embrace from the West. One direct indication of this international state of affairs is to look at the nature of the world of goods and their design. The current revival of interest in national, regional and ethnic identity might be explained as a reaction against such internationalism, as might the growth of niche-marketing.

An international chair

In many ways the furniture produced by Gebrüder Thonet after 1840 might be regarded as the epitome of early internationally-oriented industrial production. Michael Thonet (1796-1871) had developed a way of steam-bending beechwood to make furniture. The furniture was made of interchangeable parts and supplied in knock-down form. The parts were assembled by a team in a factory or by overseas wholesalers. The most famous chair made by Thonet was the 'B4' dining chair (Fig. 12).[13] Success was guaranteed when it was adopted as a standard café chair by restaurants across Europe from the 1850s. Essentially a chair for the proliferating urban middle classes, by the 1870s one factory was devoted exclusively to its production and at the height of its success 150,000 chairs were manufactured every year. Thonet's system represents an example of mass production pre-Henry Ford. Typical of Thonet's internationalism was his use of international exhibitions, extensive publicity and catalogues to sell the furniture. Thonet provided a model for much twentieth-century furniture production and distribution. As a much acclaimed example, its system was adapted by companies in Britain, Estonia, Finland and the United States, especially in the period between the two World Wars.

An international design curriculum

In 1919, Walter Gropius (1883-1969), already a well-established architect, was invited to transform the School of Arts and Crafts in Weimar, Germany for the new era. The result, the Bauhaus, an experimental school of art, design and architecture, is regarded as the most formative influence on the education of designers this century. Its example was followed internationally and the teaching and writing of its masters have been made available through extensive research and publication.[14]

The First World War had produced huge disarray. Arising from the ruins, especially in Central Europe and the new Soviet Union, came ideas of a new order: a tabula rasa for new ideals to be achieved. There was a wish to formulate designs which would not respect narrow national interests. An event such as 'The Congress of International Progressive Artists' held in Düsseldorf in 1922, which some Bauhaus figures attended, paralleled events in the wider political and social sphere, such as the foundation of the Third International of the Communist Party in 1919 and the League of Nations in 1920 (Fig. 13).

History of the Bauhaus is well-documented. The school's links with the wider field of Constructivist designers in the Soviet Union and Hungary were testimony to its international ambitions, as were the interventions of Theo van Doesburg (1883-1931), advocate of *De Stijl* principles, and the appointment of painters Paul Klee (1879-1940), a Swiss, and Wassily Kandinsky (1866-1944), a Russian, as teachers ('masters of form'). The school syllabus was revised on several occasions to accommodate the mounting concern to produce successful designs for industrial production, and after 1923 there was a move away from the use of luxury or craft materials.[15]

In 1925 Gropius oversaw the transfer of the Bauhaus to purpose-built accommodation in Dessau, a city where industrial commissions could be won (Fig. 14). The Bauhaus was closed by Nazi local government in 1932; afterwards it had short-lived revivals in Berlin and Chicago, where it was first called The New Bauhaus and subsequently the Institute of Design. The original aim was to produce architects.

12. Model B4 Chair, designer and manufacturer Michael Thonet (German, 1796-1871)
First produced in 1849
Bent beechwood with cane seat
H. 94.5 W. 41 D. 48 cm
W. 6 – 1969

Michael Thonet, who had experimented with laminated techniques from about 1830, perfected his bentwood in the 1840s, setting up a factory in 1849. This chair was first produced in a mahogany version for the celebrated Café Daum in Vienna and was still being manufactured in 1915.

13. Gropius's Office at the Weimar Bauhaus, Germany, 1923

The interior design was carried out by Walter Gropius (1883-1969) with designs by staff and students. The chair and light fittings were designed by the architect himself, the wall-hanging and carpet were made to abstract designs by the weaving workshop, and the bookcase and desk were designed by Marcel Breuer. The craft basis of many materials and techniques here might be contrasted with those in Figure 16.

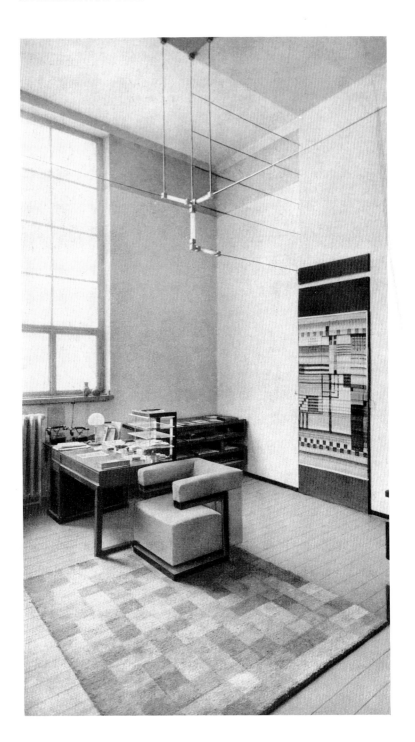

14. The Dessau Bauhaus building photographed by Lucia Moholy (British, born Prague, 1894-1989) published in *Das Werk*, Zurich, 1928

The Bauhaus moved from Weimar to Dessau and new purpose-built accommodation designed by Walter Gropius in 1925. Shown here are the student residence in a tower block with cantilevered balconies *(right)*, the refectory and lecture theatre and the staff offices *(left)*. A much celebrated building, it was included in the 1932 New York exhibition 'The International Style'.

Studios were organised according to materials. The most important feature in determining the design methodology at the school was the *Vorkurs*, a foundation course which all students were required to take. Its aim was to examine the basic vocabulary of design; to abstract principles of composition from nature; to understand materials irrespective of their application to any practical purpose; and to find general laws in line, structure, tension, composition, colour and light. Furniture was made from cantilevered aluminium, steel or glass and experimental yarns in synthetic materials were developed for fabrics (Figs. 15 and 16). Basic geometrical forms and primary colours were considered rudiments of a design language, more elemental and therefore more suitable for communication than figuration or natural colour. Graphic designs used single-case, sans-serif alphabets and mechanical composition. German industrial standards were adopted for paper sizes, paint colours and measurements of fitted furniture and building parts, not as a symptom of nationalism, but as a form of rationalisation.

Through their publication Bauhaus teaching methods were understood and applied by successive generations in design schools around the world. However, not everyone was convinced by the polemic of the protagonists. The American architect and engineer Buckminster Fuller (1895-1983) accused them of applying a superficial rather than fundamental analysis: 'The Bauhaus and International (style) used standard plumbing fixtures and only

15. The 'Wassily' chair, 1926, by Marcel Breuer (Hungarian, 1902-81), manufactured by Standard-Möbel and Breuer Metal Möbel, Germany

This photograph of a modern woman seated in a chrome armchair, named after the painter Wassily Kandinsky, encapsulated a desire to use industrial materials. In spite of many references to machine production, the chair was in fact a result of manual processes for assembly and finishing.

ventured so far as to persuade manufacturers to modify the surface of the valve handles and spigots, and the colour, size, and arrangement of the tiles. The International Bauhaus never went back of the wall-surface to look at the plumbing...they never enquired into the overall problem of sanitary fittings themselves. In short, they only looked at the problems of modifications of the surface of end-products.'[16]

'The International Style'

It was at another international setting for design in Germany's Weimar period that further ideas about Modernism became apparent; ones that would eventually be formulated under the heading of the 'International Style'. At the exhibition 'Die Wohnung' (The Dwelling) at Stuttgart in 1927, often referred to as the Weissenhof Exhibition, Gropius, Le Corbusier (Charles Edouard Jeanneret, 1887-1965), Mart Stam (1899-1986), Mies van der Rohe (1886-1969) and others contributed housing intended for use after the exhibition. Supported by the city authorities, the new buildings were supposed to be funded at the normal rate for cheap housing.[17] The contributors furnished and equipped their buildings. The critic Willi Lotz explained the new approach to the interior they adopted: 'The furniture of the houses on the Weissenhof estate in Stuttgart represented an attempt to replace matching sets of furniture, designed to go together in a room, by an assembly of individual pieces chosen from good, existing standard designs. Instead of suites of matching furniture of a similar design and made of similar materials the idea was to present the chair, the table, the bed. And, moreover, only these example were chosen which had evolved a standard design from being manufactured to functional specification...'[18]

According to this, design comprises a set of components, perceived as transferable units within their type, rather than across the species or ensemble of furniture. Characteristically for this time, Lotz did not include second-hand, inherited or antique furniture in his description. An approach such as Lotz's became an orthodoxy, shared by many designers associated with the modern tradition.

Underlying this view are two ideas which take design away from

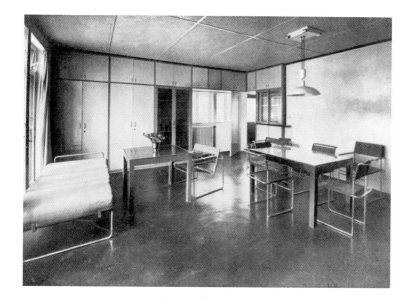

16. The Living-Dining Room, Gropius Haus, Dessau, Germany, 1928

The house was designed by Walter Gropius and the interior arranged by his Bauhaus colleague, Marcel Breuer. It included a glass-top table, a day bed and chrome dining chairs by Breuer and a pendant lamp by M. Brandt and H. Przyrembel of the metal workshops. Other features which were to be recognised as part of the International Style were the clear floor plan and lack of applied decoration.

specific, culturally-produced meaning to more general or universal properties in design. The first is a neo-Kantian search for absolutes in everyday objects, not *any* chair but *the* definitive.[19] This approach to design greatly valued abstraction of form. Inherent was the belief that 'specifications' of industrial production were more systematic and less susceptible to variation, artistic will or temperament. If the chair is definitive, then it follows it would be successful internationally.

A second, related idea used by Lotz and many of his contemporaries was informed by evolutionary theory. He argued that useful objects evolve towards an optimum form. Le Corbusier had already suggested the Bordeaux wine bottle and the briar pipe were 'type-objects'; anonymous industrial objects which had reached their simplest and most functional form (Fig. 17).[20] Both arguments were popular and formative in their time and more recently have been used to support the notion of timeless 'classics' of design.

During the 1920s in New York, the Metropolitan Museum of Art held exhibitions on the subject of Industrial Art. The Museum of Modern Art (MoMA) in New York, founded in 1929, opened its Department of Industrial Design in 1933. The first design-related exhibitions were 'Machine Art' of 1934 and 'Bauhaus 1919-28' of

17. 'The Aesthetic of the Engineer', an article from *L'Esprit Nouveau*, nos 10-13, Paris 1922, edited by Le Corbusier (Charles Édouard Jeanneret, Swiss, 1887-1966) and Amedée Ozenfant (French, 1886-1966)

This article, a rallying call to supporters of the 'new spirit', contrasted the 'painful regression' of architecture with the 'full flowering' of engineering. The latter was illustrated by a viaduct by Eiffel, grain silos in Canada and industrial wharfs.

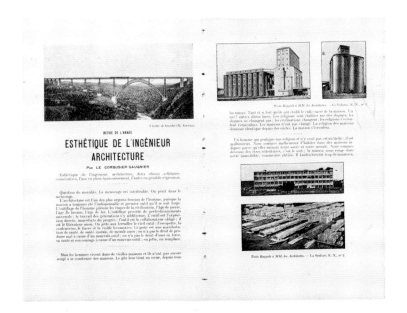

1938.[21] After the Second World War, MoMA became an arbiter of taste, giving design awards to selected product and industrial designs in a manner similar to the European Design Councils.

In 1932, 'Modern Architecture – International Exhibition' opened at MoMA, marking the original use of the term 'International Style' applied to the new architecture.[22] The exhibition contained models, drawings and photographs of work by Mies van der Rohe, Le Corbusier, Frank Lloyd Wright, J.J.P. Oud, Walter Gropius, the Bowman brothers, Richard Neutra and Raymond Hood, mainly collected after a European tour made by the organisers, art historian Henry Russell Hitchcock and architect Philip Johnson. Although largely an architectural exhibition, many of the contributors were designing furniture and their interiors were considered some of the most significant of the time.[23]

Design as international business

'In his room stood an American writing-desk of superior construction, such as his father had coveted for years and tried to pick up at all sorts of auction sales without ever succeeding, his resources being much too small. This desk, of course, was beyond all comparison with the so-called American writing-desk which turned up at auction sales in Europe. For example, it had a hundred compartments of different sizes, in which the President of the Union himself could have found a fitting place for each of his state documents; there was also a regulator at one side and by turning a handle you could produce the most complicated combinations and permutations of the compartments to please yourself and suit your requirements. Thin panels sank slowly and formed the bottom of a new series or the top of existing drawers promoted from below; even after one turn of the handle the position of the whole was quite changed and the transformation took place slowly or at delirious speed according to the rate at which you wound the thing round. It was a very modern invention, yet it reminded Karl vividly of the traditional panorama which was shown to gaping children in the market-place at home...' Franz Kafka (1883-1924).[24]

An alternative, commercially buoyant and optimistic internationalism arose from the United States. By the 1930s it had forced other leading nations to reconsider their interpretations of design practice. Characteristically, it was enhanced by a belief in the creative individual in the form of the industrial designer. Recent years have witnessed a substantial increase in the literature on this early American industrial history. The most formative study, *Mechanization Takes Command*, might in many ways be seen as a response to the distinctive traditions of the United States.[25] Its author, the architectural critic Siegfried Giedion (1888-1968), a Swiss, resident in the United States from 1941 to 1945, addressed the role of mechanisation not just in systems of manufacture but also in the home. His perspective was to consider anonymous artefacts which had influenced the principal aspects of people's lives.

Subsequent studies have isolated the particular character of American industrial organisation.[26] Modern American design arose more from increased division of labour and the need to be commercially effective, less from a search by artists, architects and designers for an abstract quality grounded in idealist aesthetics as had occurred in Europe. Concerning production between 1820 and 1840, Arthur Pulos has suggested: 'The concept of design as a means by which a

18. End of the Line, Ford Factory, Highland Park, USA, 1913

Henry Ford introduced a moving line system of chassis assembly in 1907 for the production of the first successful low-price motor-car. The Model T ran from 1908-1927 and was available in black only. It was rapidly celebrated as the epitome of the American system of manufacture.

19. Henry Ford and Edsel B. Ford, with the new Model A Ford in December 1927, on the first public showing at the Waldorf Hotel, New York

With increasing competition from other automobile manufacturers, Henry Ford conceded that a new model for a low cost vehicle was required to maintain Ford's market share. The Model A was available in varied colours, with design changes introduced to the radiator grill and fender, signalling a move to flexible standardisation.

plan for a product could be conceived in the mind and laid out in detail for analysis and evaluation before it was manufactured began to expand the traditional use of the word design beyond artistic composition and decoration.'[27]

The most famous industrial model of production this century, Henry Ford's system for automobiles, depended on continuous progression of the product through the factory. Assemblers and mechanics remained in one place while the products passed them on the production line (Fig. 18). This was believed to achieve the shortest time for assembly while causing minimum fatigue. A plant would operate a 24-hour day organised according to three eight-hour shifts. Under such a system, 15 million 'Model T' Fords were eventually produced.[28]

Design differentiation entered the production and distribution equation in 1927, when Ford conceded that a change in a car's style might help its sales against competition from other car manufacturers, most notably General Motors, and introduced the 'Model A' (Fig. 19). No doubt at the level of popular understanding and the construction of a national identity, 'Fordism' was hugely influential as a hallmark of Americanisation, with its connotations of plenty and efficiency. Nevertheless it is debatable how extensively the American system was adopted, when subsidiaries were set up in other countries. Many industries in Europe were not equipped to move to Ford-type mass production, whereas many other industries, such as Olivetti typewriters or Morris cars, were.[29]

Central to a history of American design are consumer durable products such as typewriters, telephones, refrigerators and many other products associated with modern everyday life. Although such items were also made in Europe, often by American subsidiaries, America took the lead. The many examples of international con-vergence show how quickly other countries took to 'Americanisation'. Initially such products were conceived by engineers, but their appearance was transformed during the boom years of the 1920s in the United States in the hands of the 'industrial designer'.

The American system of production meant no shortage of goods.

20 a and 20 b.
The 'Gestetner model
66 Duplicator', before
and after remodelling by
Raymond Loewy (French,
1893-1986), and made
by Gestetner Ltd, UK
Wood and metal,
H. 31 W. 61 D. 38cm
and base.
W. 47 – 1981

This is an early example
of a consultant designer
applying a streamlined
appearance to an existing
industrial product. Loewy
transformed the shape by
covering the existing model
in clay to mould a new
form reminiscent of a
skyscraper. Loewy asked
for three days and $2,000
for his services.

Instead, a need arose for product differentiation to avoid saturation of the market, even before the Wall Street Crash of 1929. Commentators have suggested that the most obvious route to becoming an industrial designer in the American context was through graphic design and advertising. It was a short step from drawing an idealised product for the page of a magazine to designing a real industrial object. From supplying trademarks designers moved to producing advertisement designs and marketing strategies, then to styling the product itself. The story of Raymond Loewy is instructive in this connection (Figs. 20 and 21): 'The Gestetner duplicating machine, 1929, is generally considered the first example of industrial design before industrial design was understood as a conscious activity…It deserves attention for another reason: it points out the difference between a straight engineering approach and the designer's attitude when faced with the same problem – in this particular case note the four protruding tubular supports. As a consumer-conscious designer, I detected the inherent hazards of the four protruding legs in a busy office. While my client, Sigmund Gestetner, seemed hesitant about giving me the re-design assignment, I quickly sketched a stenographer tripping over a leg, paper flying everywhere. This sold him, and I got the job. During the early days of industrial design, I often used a rough-sketch device to promote what we could do for the client.'[30]

The Hollywood star-system could be applied to designers just as much as to film actors. Their professionalisation was advanced by publishing autobiographical accounts; the first of this genre was Norman Bel Geddes' *Horizons* of 1932. Another indication of their increased status was in the setting up of various professional bodies; the first, in 1938, was the Chicago-based American Designers' Institute, later called the Industrial Designers' Institute, while in New York the Society of Industrial Designers was established in 1944.

External perceptions of 'America' were constantly fuelled by the romance associated with the film industry, Manhattan skyscrapers, streamlining and vast open spaces: a place for pioneers (Figs. 22 and 23). New materials contributed to this; plastics production nearly doubled between 1935 and the outbreak of the Second World War.

21. Raymond Loewy (left) with the President of the Pennsylvania Railroad Co. in front of their offices in Philadelphia, USA, 1935

Loewy applied the same styling to office interiors, publicity and trademarks and industrial products. He introduced streamlining to America's rail transport systems. In his drawings for the S.I. locomotive in 1937, for instance, Loewy separated the outer shell from the internal mechanism to achieve a seamless appearance.

By 1940 a leading business magazine, *Fortune*, could describe a plastic 'American Dream of Venus': 'Dentures, door-knobs, gears, goggles, juke boxes, crystal chairs, transparent shoes and ladies rise up from the plastic sea.'[31]

Most nations were susceptible to the allure of 'Americanisation', which was sustained as a consumer dream into the 1960s. It is perhaps worth considering how man-made materials, apparently with less hierarchy and history than natural substances, contributed to this self-conscious identity. Was it a construction used to forge a national identity for the culturally diverse populations of this New World, just as much as a successful attempt to secure markets in the rest of the world?

22. Furnishing
Fabric: Manhattan.
Designed by Ruth Reeves
(American, 1892-1966)
Made by W. & J. Sloane,
New York City, USA, 1930
Block printed cotton voile
T. 57 – 1932

Reeves studied in
Brooklyn, New York, and
with Fernand Léger in
Paris. This design shows
the influences of both.
Symbols of modernity –
transport, engineering,
architecture and
communications
technology – are linked
by Cubist-inspired
compositional devices
to create a romantic
vision of Manhattan.

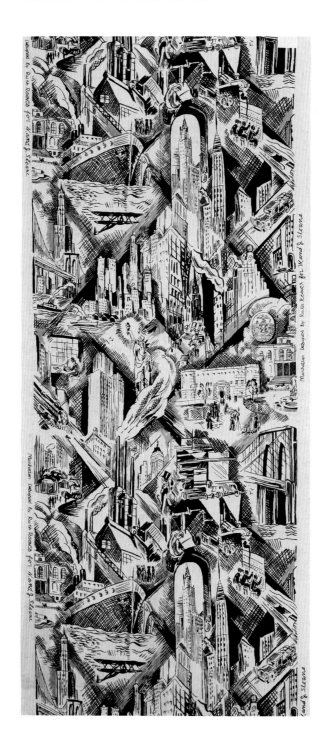

23. Photograph of
the new Empire State
Building, New York,
Fred Zinnemann
(Austrian, b. 1909) 1932
Gelatin silver print
E. 1674 – 1989

Zinnemann first arrived
in New York in October
1929, on Black Thursday,
the day Wall Street
crashed. In his photographs
he concentrated on the
skyline and buildings of
Manhattan, helping to
establish the cultural
identity of New York.

Nationalism

National style

'A nation is an historically evolved, stable community of language, territory, economic life and psychological make-up manifested in a community of culture.' Joseph Stalin (1879-1953)[32]

There has long been an interest in identifying national characteristics in design and manufacture. Geography has naturally played a part in the way in which people identify aspects of culture: to attach them to a town, region or a country often says something else about the materials we expect to see; the stylistic or figurative traditions associated with the place; or possibly even the cost. Apart from distinctions drawn by the geography of design, it has been commonplace to classify artistic and design production of specific historical periods by stylistic labels.[33] For instance, terms such as 'Mannerism', 'Baroque', 'Rococo', or the various 'isms' of twentieth-century experimental and avant-garde movements, 'Futurism', 'Purism' and 'Constructivism', derive from the assumption that the cultural production of specific historical periods can be grouped according to stylistic attributes and assembled in a taxonomy. However, even within this kind of classification, commentators are often keen to differentiate geographically, for instance between 'South German' and 'Roman' Baroque, 'Italian' Futurism and 'Russian' Futurism, or to define 'Czech' Cubism against 'French' Cubism (Figs. 24 and 25).[34]

In the book *Objects of Desire – Design and Society 1750-1980*, Adrian Forty presented the case that emphasis on the individual designer in histories of design can be a distorting and inaccurate interpretation of how many industrially-produced objects actually come into being.[35] Instead, Forty suggests that the way things look arises from wider economic, social and political forces which impinge on objects. Designers are part of, rather than separate from, this complex world and we cannot expect them to design without such forces affecting the results. This view of the designer and design process helps in understanding national meanings.

24. Plate, 'The Seamstress', designed by Alexandr Nikolaevich Samokhvalov (Russian, 1894-1971), made at the State Porcelain Factory, Leningrad, Russia in 1923 and decorated 1924. Porcelain, painted decoration Misc. 2 (59) – 1934

Following the 1917 October Revolution, modern Russian artists were placed in factories to provide designs and decorations. The subject-matter had social meaning and the decoration combined a strong realist flavour with facetting from Futurism, considered by its advocates as an appropriate and progressive language for the new Communist order.

25. Villa in Vysehrad, Prague, 1911-12 designed by Josef Chochol (Czech, 1880-1956), photographed in 1991

Unlike French Cubism, which resulted in only one projected building, the Maison Cubiste, Czech designers and architects applied new aesthetic theories inspired by Einstein's ideas of a dynamic reality and the experimental crystalline form in buildings, graphic arts, furniture, glass and ceramics.

26. Lampshades designed by Isamu Noguchi (Japanese, 1904-1988)

A range of Akari light sculptures on display in Area 13 of the Isamu Noguchi Garden Museum in Long Island City.

National style, it would appear, usually does not arise from a single designer's intention to work according to a country's traditions. Instead, attitudes, beliefs and knowledge are established through education and media, promoted in exhibitions and museums, and receive encouragement from government, industry and influential individuals. More straightforwardly, the economy of a nation will have an impact on the path of successful design, as the emigration of design ideas from one country and their development in another often proves. However, when considering a nation's design traditions, we encounter connotations and associations which depend on stereotypical as well as accurate perceptions. The French writer Roland Barthes (1915-1980) developed a theory of semiology, or 'science of signs', which may be useful in explaining how national characteristics can be encoded in everyday objects or representations. One of the subjects Barthes analysed was an Italian food advertisement intended for French readers.[36]

There have always been successful designs which have managed to incorporate sufficient qualities for them to be taken up as national icons. The 'Akari' lantern, a lampshade originally made from bamboo and rice paper, designed by the sculptor Isamu Noguchi (1904-1988), is one such example (Fig. 26). Its imagery and materials offer a conflation of meaning: Japan's national symbol is the rising sun, while 'Akari' means 'illumination' in Japanese. Bamboo and handmade paper, the materials in the original version of the lamp, are part of the essential construction of a traditional Japanese house, and the lantern also refers to folk lanterns (Fig. 27).[37] As well as incorporating this national significance, it has been reworked by manufacturers as an effective and affordable commodity in many parts of the world. Its concertina structure allows it to be flat-packed and the apparent neutrality of its design makes it adaptable to many types of room furnishings in various cultures.

National formations of design

The balance of power in Europe changed considerably in the second half of the nineteenth century when competition between forms of national cultural and industrial production increased. Italy completed its *Risorgimento* by the act of unification in 1870. The German states were unified in 1871. As a new nation, Germany's strength in raw materials, production of iron and steel, and emergent electrical and chemical dyestuff industries, signalled a new international power. Vienna, capital of the Austrian part of Austria-Hungary, flourished between 1880 and 1914 in the area of arts and crafts, theatre and music. By 1900, the map of Europe looked quite different from thirty years before and the traditional great powers, Britain and France, found the newer nation states presenting a formidable challenge.[38]

The wealth of nations was defined by prowess in industrial production, which came to be valued in new terms of efficiency and design, as well as in the more conventional ones of cost of raw materials and labour. The British Government took a significant step towards helping to define these new interests in 1835-1836 when a Select Committee on Arts and Manufacture was established to discuss the training of apprentices and the future workforce. National Schools of Design were established as a result of their recommendations in 1848 and these were directly comparable with schools in France, Prussia and Bavaria. At this time, Prince Albert, acting as the President of the Society of Arts, recommended that Britain follow the example of France in holding exhibitions of

27. A traditional Japanese house

On the horizontal plane the arrangement of the traditional Japanese house is determined by the *tatami*, a finely-woven straw mat. Vertically, the walls, sliding doors and movable partitions are made of paper on light wooden frames. While constituting a national tradition, the aesthetic and functional clarity of these houses also inspired many Modern Movement architects and designers.

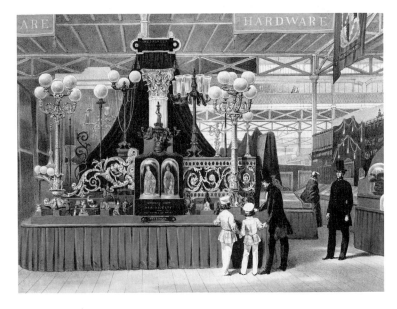

28. Hand-coloured lithograph, H. C. Pidgeon (1807-1880) 'Part of the Birmingham Court' in the Crystal Palace, Hyde Park. From *Recollection of the Great Exhibition*,1851, published by Lloyd Brothers and Co. and Simpkin, Marshall and Co., London, 1851 38 x 29.4 cm DP&D 19538 – 12

The Great Exhibition served as a feast for the eye, combining manufactured goods and raw materials in vast cast-iron and glass structures. In turn, it anticipated the parades of items on display in the new department stores and museums. The experience of visiting the Exhibition therefore combined the instruction of the public both as consumers and as students.

industrial art. Instead of the large national French exhibitions, the proposed London version was to have international contributions. Under the headings 'raw materials', 'machinery and mechanical inventions', 'manufactures' and 'the plastic arts' contributions were invited from across the world. The Great Exhibition of 1851 held in the Crystal Palace in Hyde Park became the model for a century of international exhibitions (Figs. 28 and 29).[39]

On this platform of international competition, individual countries had the opportunity to perceive their products' strengths and weaknesses in a much more direct manner than the systems of sales between countries based on individual markets had previously allowed. The encouragement of national identity was an inevitable by-product of such events, stoked by the wish to further define identity with yet more sophisticated layers of propaganda and persuasion.

Most governments encouraged the foundation of national museums of decorative and applied art in the latter part of the nineteenth century. The first of these, the South Kensington Museum, later called the Victoria and Albert Museum, was established following the 1851 Great Exhibition, as a repository for the exhibits. Its original stated purpose was for the instruction and improvement of

29. Photograph of the Worth fashion house display, Exposition Universelle, Paris, 1900

Worth's display at the Paris Universal Exhibition consisted of a tableau 'Going to the Drawing Room'. It combined a conspicuous display of the latest luxury fashions with correct notions of deportment and manners, possibly for emulation. Such scenes were reminiscent of the illustrated pages of high-quality fashion magazines, another forum for international comparison.

design for manufacture. Vienna followed with its Arts and Crafts Museum in 1864. Berlin's Kunstgewerbemuseum started as a private foundation in 1867 and became the Royal Decorative Art and Design Museum in 1879. In Paris, the Union Central des Beaux Arts Appliqués à l'Industrie was formed, 'to counter threats posed to French trade and manufacturers by improving English standards of design'.[40] By 1882 its work culminated in the formation of the Musée des Arts Décoratifs in the Palais de l'Industrie.

The terms on which the national museums of applied and decorative arts collected their artefacts were highly influenced by the writings of John Ruskin (1819-1900) and William Morris (1834-96). These authors' most consistent criticism had contrasted commercially-led industrial manufacture, organised around alienated labour, with the fulfilling handwork of medieval times.[41] The museums would display objects of highly skilled craftmanship, historical examples as well as contemporary products and commissions, for the instruction of industry, often through schools attached to these institutions (Fig. 30). The art and industry debate carried across Germany, Central Europe and Russia and to smaller countries such as Belgium, the Netherlands and to some extent Scandinavia, where it was

30. The Museum of Applied Arts, Budapest, Hungary, designed by Edmund (Ödön) Lechner (1845-1914) with Bela Partos, 1893-96. Photograph by Bruno Reiffenstein, Vienna, 1928

This National Museum was the first building in Hungary in which Lechner mixed folk references with oriental decorative motifs, employing highly-coloured ceramic tiles of Zsolnay Majolika. This free Gothic style was associated with the Hungarian National Romantic movement at the turn of the century.

subsumed in a wave of National Romanticism.[42] The United States, Italy and France, with their distinct craft and handwork traditions, held different attitudes to the Arts and Crafts reforms: 'Ruskin and Morris strove to find a means of reuniting the world of art with the world of work. Towards the end of the century their lead was followed by Van de Velde, Olbrich, Behrens and others on the Continent. This movement which started with the building of the 'Artists' Colony' at Darmstadt and culminated in the founding of the Deutscher Werkbund in Munich, led to the establishment of the Kunstgewerbeschulen in the principal German towns. These were intended to give the rising generation of artists and designers a practical training for handicrafts and industry.'[43]

Closely allied to the movement to establish national museums was the formation of professional associations of industrialists concerned with the encouragement of 'good' design for industry. The first of these was the Deutscher Werkbund, established in Munich in 1907.[44] Through its meetings, publications and exhibitions, notions of good practice were disseminated. The German Werkbund was distinctive among such associations in relating the issue to industrial production rather than craft reform, reconciling the fissure that

31. Decanter designed by
Charles Robert Ashbee
(British, 1863-1942) made
by the Guild of Handicraft
Ltd, Chipping Campden,
Gloucestershire, 1904-5
Green glass, silver,
chrysoprase.
W. 16¹/₂ H. 22¹/₂ cm
M. 121 – 1966

The wish to incorporate
indigenous patterns in many
Arts and Crafts designs
indicated a respect for pre-
industrial crafts. The form
of this decanter is based
on an English sixteenth
century sack bottle.
Ashbee established a co-
operative of craftspeople
in London in 1888 which
subsequently moved to
Chipping Campden,
Gloucestershire in 1902.

32. *Deutscher Werkbund Jahrbuch*, 1912
Published by Eugen Diederichs, Jena, Germany, 1912

Two pages from the yearbook of the German Werkbund with displays of kettles and table-lamps by A. Sonnenschein *(left)* and a tea service and cutlery by Henry van de Velde *(right)*. By contrast with Fig.31 these objects were of industrial manufacture intended for home and overseas markets.

Morris and Ruskin had identified, and in part, produced (Figs. 31 and 32). One of the aims of the Werkbund was to advise the government on new designs and to guide it away from historicism. A prominent founding member, the architect Hermann Muthesius (1861-1927), for example, was responsible for administering the 'Prussian System of Technical Standards', which, as John Heskett has suggested, was an effective way to use aesthetic means to establish a national culture.[45] Following the example of Germany, the Austrians and Swiss established their own associations for art and industry, named after the Werkbund, in 1910 and 1913 respectively.

The Arts and Crafts Exhibition Society had promoted work produced within the Guilds according to the ideals of Morris. However, a British organisation which embraced industrial design, the Design and Industries Association, was formed in 1915, after a group of its founding members had visited the highly significant 'Deutscher Werkbund' exhibition held in Cologne in 1914 (Fig. 33).[46]

Germany's increasingly prestigious position as an industrial nation acted as a catalyst for many countries' moves towards design reform. On the competition between Germany and France, the historian Nancy Troy has shown how 'Die Ausstellung' in Munich in 1908, a large display organised to boast the achievements of the South

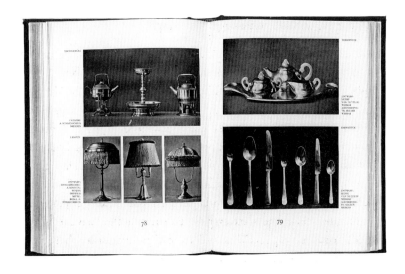

German Workshop Movement, warned French furniture trades that they should not take for granted their assumed pre-eminence in the field of design.[47] By 1908 the French noticed that German workshops were adopting a more industrially-attuned model, prompted no doubt by the debates within Werkbund circles, and this was confirmed in the 1910 Brussels exhibition where: 'The fact that many of the objects in these well-orchestrated ensembles had not been executed solely for the purpose of the exhibition but were available for purchase in several shops in the city further testified to the practical rather than strictly artistic orientation of the Munich designers.'[48]

Here, distinct national differences were apparent, based on each state's attitude towards promotion of the furniture industries. The French had a long tradition of the *artiste-décorateur*, which encouraged an exclusive system to be run on the lines of the other Fine Arts: a *Salon*, a studio workshop system and strict copyright laws on designs, the signatures on the pieces distinguishing them from industrial objects (Figs. 34 and 35). On seeing the contrast between the two countries' displays in Paris in 1911, the French art critic Louis Vauxcelles wrote: 'I declare it with despair, we do not have the least bit of discipline, not the least bit of method. Think of the cohesion manifested by those people of Munich! Their teams (of workmen) marched at parade pace. We may be charming and witty, but we frolic about in ultra-dispersed array.'[49]

If we take a wider scenario than the politics of furniture, such writing indicates how national stereotypes can be combined with critical judgement. In fact, individual designs shown by German contributors still owed a great deal to the Viennese workshop movement, considered stylistically superior by many German critics. Therefore it cannot just be seen as a straightforward national tradition (Fig. 36).[50] The full impact of this national competition was to come to a dreadful culmination in the outbreak of the First World War, which significantly altered the next generation's perceptions. To a great extent it determined the drive towards international co-operation, and investigations into shared, as opposed to competitive, approaches to design.

33. *Trend in Design*, no. 1, Spring 1936, the official quarterly of the Design and Industries Association, London

This publication, like its German and Swedish predecessors, was intended to guide British consumers and industrialists in thinking about 'good design'. It included contributions from HM King Edward VIII and well-known design reformers, Frank Pick, Kenneth Clark, William Crawford and Sir Stephen Tallents.

34. Dressing Table and Stool designed by Emile-Jacques Ruhlmann (French, 1879-1933), made by Établissements Ruhlmann et Laurent, Paris, France, about 1919. Purple heart (amaranth), mahogany, ivory and ebony on an oak carcase; silver bronze mirror frame and fittings. Table H. 121.3 W. 76.2 x D. 52.1 cm W. 14, 15 – 1980

The shape of the dressing table is derived from the French Empire style but it is simpler than its nineteenth-century predecessors. Its intricate and illusionistic use of ivory inlay and ebony is a demonstration of the French luxury tradition of furniture which was celebrated at the 1925 Paris Exposition des Arts Décoratifs.

35. A dining room designed by Richard Riemerschmid (German, 1868-1957), Munich, and made by the Deutsche Werkstätten, GmbH, Hellerau, Dresden, Germany. From *Deutschlands Raumkunst und Kunstgewerbe auf der Weltausstellung in Brüssel*, published by Julius Hoffmann Verlag, Stuttgart 1910

In the rooms on display at this exhibition, the idea of 'Types' was advanced by many of the German contributors. According to this, form and decoration should be appropriate to the function of the room. Riemerschmid gained commissions for the design of ship interiors which encouraged him to think about interchangeable units and standard sizes.

The first professional design associations were conceived by industrialists and their design allies to promote the use of designers within industry and were an integral part of the early formation of national cultures. A second series of organisations was formed in the mid-twentieth century. These were national Design Councils. While still concerned to promote a nation's industry abroad, their emphasis was on design education as an essential element in a modern social democracy. Accordingly, it is perhaps not surprising that Modernism was often assumed to be the natural artistic form to secure state approval. To take the example of Britain: on the outbreak of the Second World War in 1939, a Government initiative to sustain cultural life until peace returned led to the formation of the Committee for the Encouragement of Arts and Music (CEMA).[51] In 1944, the Council of Industrial Design was established by the President of the Board of Trade, to aid in the production and marketing of British goods. The COID published the magazine *Design* from 1949 and opened Design Centres in London and Glasgow, changing its name to the Design Council in 1972 (Fig. 37). In the years of post-war reconstruction, parallel developments can be noticed in other countries. For example, the 'Design Council' of the Federal Republic of Germany was formed under Mia Seeger in 1953 and a Design Centre founded in Stuttgart in 1962. In the German Democratic Republic a 'Council of Industrial Form' (*Rat für Formgebung*) was established in 1962; a 'Good Design' prize was introduced in 1978 and a Design Centre opened in 1987 in East Berlin.[52] International recognition of industrial

36. Writing Desk and Chair designed by Kolomon Moser (Austrian, 1868-1918), made by Caspar Hrazdil, Vienna, Austria, 1903. Thuya wood, inlaid with satinwood and brass, engraved and inked; gilt metal feet; mahogany interior oak lining drawer, deal carcase. Desk, H. 1450cm W. 1190 D. 596cm W. 8 & a – 1982

This desk was part of a total decorative scheme commissioned for an apartment in Vienna and dates from the year the Werkstätte were founded. The repeated geometric motifs of the ornament became characteristic of the Viennese style.

37. 'Improving Standards in Northern Ireland', from an article in *Design* magazine, London, July 1965

This exhibition in Northern Ireland, the largest CoID exhibition outside London, represented 212 firms from the United Kingdom and 30 firms from Northern Ireland. Visitors averaged 1,820 per day.

38. 'Lathörnet': an illustration from the book *Ett Hem* (A Home) by Carl Larsson (Swedish, 1853-1919). Published by A. Bonniers, Sweden, 1899

A popular success in Sweden and Germany, Larsson depicted his home in watercolours which integrated folk simplicity with neo-classical furniture. The books were instilled with a concern for nature, domesticity and appropriate decoration which would become hallmarks of a 'Swedish' approach to design.

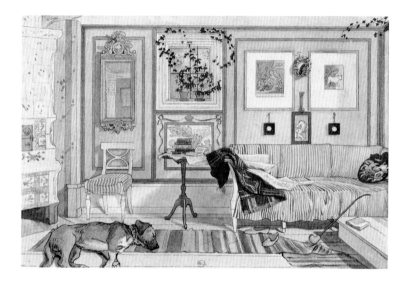

39. Part of a dinner service, 'Liljeblå' (Blue Lily), designed by Wilhelm Kåge (Swedish, 1889-1960), and made by Gustavsberg, Sweden, 1917. Earthenware with grey-blue glaze and printed decoration. C. 190-b – 1986

Kåge, a painter by training, joined the Gustavsberg company as art director in 1917. The Blue Lily was also known as the 'worker's service' and was a deliberate attempt to produce an inexpensive service which was characteristic of the social idealism of modern design in Sweden, as promoted by Svenska Föreningen.

design was reached with the formation of ICSID, the International Council of Societies of Industrial Design, in 1959, linking leading professional organisations worldwide.

The case of Scandinavia

The collective identity of Norway, Denmark, Sweden, Finland, later joined by Iceland, has often been conceived as a 'third way', defined by their strong traditions of social democracy, poised between communism and capitalism. These countries pioneered successful forms of national intervention in town planning, building and design for manufacture: capitalism with a benign face. Similarly, their design traditions have been regarded as successful adaptations of foreign traditions, sensitively fused with national strengths: Modernism with a human face. Interestingly, in the Scandinavian case, design traditions preceded political ones. Following Gramsci's ideas, this may be a case where political economy grew out of cultural activity.[53]

The countries can be typified by a shared design idealism: an ambition to achieve good quality products and a belief in a democratic household culture, in which tableware, textiles, ceramics and glass played a most significant part. This was deemed important because of the centrality of the home for everyday life in

40. Armchair Model 41 designed by Alvar Aalto (Finnish, 1898-1976), 1930 and manufactured by Oy. Huonekalu-ja Rakennus-tyotehdas AB, Turku, 1932-35, and later by Artek, Helsinki, Finland. Birch plywood and solid birch with painted seat.
H. 63.5cm W. 61cm
D. 89cm
W. 41 – 1987

Aalto can be placed among the Functionalist group. Although he designed chairs which combined plywood and steel, he grew to feel that metal was too harsh for the interior. He looked to the abundant birch forests of his native land for his raw material.

41. Vase and stand, 'Fyverkerlskålen' (Fireworks Bowl), designed by Edward Hald (Swedish, 1883-1980), 1921, and made by Orrefors, Sweden 1930; engraved by Karl Rossler.
Diameter 27.6 cm
Circ. 52 and A – 1931

This vase was exhibited at the Stockholm exhibition in 1930 and the 'Exhibition of Swedish Industrial Art' held at Dorland Hall in London, 1931. Hald and other designers represented a tendency in Swedish design which combined classicism and French modern art, dubbed 'Swedish Grace' by the English critic, Morton Shand.

42. Book, *Building Modern Sweden* by Bertil Hultén, Penguin Books, Harmondsworth 1951. Designed by Erik Frederiksen, photographs by C. G. Rosenberg

The successful blend of social democracy and modern design made Sweden a place of pilgrimage for many architects and designers in the 1940s and 1950s.

the short daylight hours of winter. Commentators usually agree that a search for beauty was resolved in the close association between organic forms and natural materials in Scandinavian design (Fig. 38). In 1900, at the Paris Exposition, the Nordic contribution was noticed: 'In these remote countries a powerful art movement is forcing its way into the general art development of Europe and…it will undoubtedly ere long, claim greater public attention.'[54]

In 1917, the Swedish Design Reform Society (Svensk Föreningen, now called Svensk Form) saw its role as: 'To bring about improvements in the products of Swedish handicraft and industry through cooperation with artistic forces, better the household culture and work to raise the general level of taste.'[55]

A key to Scandinavian success was the placement of professionally-trained artists in the studios of the main art industries for glass, ceramics and stainless steel (Fig. 39). This policy was embraced by industries, which recognised the benefits of design for their main commercial range as well as prestigious studio lines. The design debate was not, however, without tensions. For example, these erupted during the 1920s and 1930s between those interested in the luxury and tradition orientation of the art industries and those of a more functionalist tendency, called 'Funkis'. Even within the Functionalist group, ideas from Soviet Constructivism or German Modernism were adapted and 'softened' using indigenous timber, glass and abundant steel (Figs. 40 and 41).

During the 1950s the distinction between individual countries in the Scandinavian 'group of five' was lost and the general term 'Scandinavian Design' fostered for overseas consumption. A sequence of successful exhibitions in other parts of Europe, but especially North America, helped reinforce this identity. As a result, the British Design Council, for example, encouraged visits by designers and architects to learn from their Nordic neighbours (Fig. 42).[56] In other circles the Scandinavian 'look' came to be regarded as over-serious and restrictive, especially with the challenge presented by Pop and the advent of Italian design. This criticism was confronted by designers of the next generation, who introduced elements not at first associated with their countries' designs: references to Nordic mythology, primitivism, high colour, wit and humour, breaking the historic mould of Scandinavian 'good form'(Fig. 43).

Nationalist design

One of the clearest instances of design being used as part of a nationalist ideological strategy was during the Third Reich in Germany, from 1933 to 1945. This sensitive period in history is open to further research because of the general difficulties it posed for historians following 1945 and, consequently, a comprehensive secondary source in English has yet to be written.[57] After the election to power of Adolf Hitler in January 1933, a reactive cultural policy pushed art, design and architecture, as well as film, to the forefront of a propaganda initiative. Under the administration of the Reich Minister for Propaganda and Enlightenment, Joseph Goebbels (1897-1945), a cultural realignment (*Gleichschaltung*) took place, whereby Jewish, Modernist and Communist practitioners were removed from office, forced to emigrate or undergo internal migration. Industrial and craft design (*Handwerk*) were organised into cultural chambers. The organisation Beauty of Work (*Schönheit der Arbeit*) under the auspices of the German Work League (*Deutsche Arbeitsfront*) carried through legislation and organised the 'correct' national mode of production, controlling styles, materials and techniques, conveyed through propaganda (Fig. 44). A parallel reform of art and design teaching took place.

The National Socialist policy for industrial production was technocratic: a large state run industrial production aimed to put expansionist Germany on a war-footing. Design for domestic consumption was not a priority, though nonetheless there was a need to provide examples of German goods for exhibition and propaganda use (Fig. 45).[58]

In official designs, Neo-classicism was the preferred architectural style and decoration, while for less official buildings and interiors, a 'German' vernacular was advocated. This policy offered spurious arguments for the origins of certain forms to make the case that they were 'national', given a '*völkisch*', culturally-conservative

43. Figure 'Kärleksgudinna' (Lovelady), designed and decorated by Ulrica Hydman-Vallien (Swedish, b.1938), Glass blown by Håkon Gunnarsson and Mikael Svensson Kosta; made at Kosta Boda, Sweden, 1986. Handblown glass, handpainted with coloured enamels.
H. 58.5 cm
C. 106 – 1988

A sculptural rather than functional use of glass made for the exhibition 'Kosta Boda sixth sense' in Stockholm, 1986. This is one of a group of figures, 'Islanders' which the maker has described as 'the strong and loving woman that dares to be proud of her self and her strong expressions and to keep the men close, and she has the nasty smile - between the smile of a madonna and a witch'.

44. Commemorative map of the Nuremburg rally, Germany, 1935, designed by A. Mahlau

This map, used for the 'Party Day of Freedom' rally at Nuremburg, shows an anti-modern, medievalising and heraldic design which was intended to instil a sense of national consciousness in the German people. In the previous year this event was recorded in the most modern medium, by Leni Riefenstahl's film 'The Triumph of the Will'.

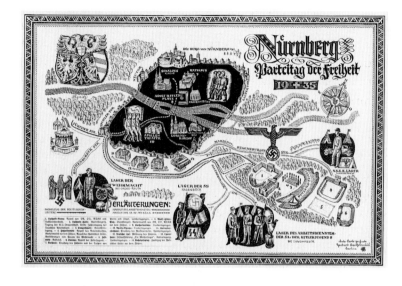

45. Photograph of the installation of the First International Craft Exhibition in Berlin from *Die Kunst im Dritten Reich* (Art in the Third Reich), Munich, July 1937

This exhibition exemplified the particular mixture of Neo-classical setting and handmade artifacts which became a characteristic of official National Socialist policy. The commentary stressed how the display of ceramics, dress, furniture, textiles and tools could reinforce national culture in reaction to the 'one-sided objectivity' and technical priorities of the democratic years.

justification. For instance, as is well known, the official typeface used was blackletter Gothic, which was advocated as a 'German' letterform with its origins in the days of Gutenberg (Johann Gensfleisch zum Gutenberg, c.1387-1486). However, this was often supplemented by Roman typefaces, partly to render German printed material legible for foreign readers.

In furniture, the new designs of the Weimar Republic were often dismissed as tainted by Bolshevism, considered inappropriate for a German home or ridiculed as factory art. In official contexts, forms and materials were chosen which stressed *Handwerk* skills of the German craftsman, and designs were historicist and conservative in taste. For interior decorative schemes the wish to employ indigenous raw materials saw, for example, an abundance of wrought ironwork and woven hangings featuring heraldic or folk patterns (Fig. 46). A review of *The Studio* or other contemporary decorative art and design journals reveals that such interiors were not exclusively the province of German taste at this time.[58] In many countries a reaction against international modern styles had set in by the mid 1930s. However, the commentaries or 'reports' of National Socialist official party publications which gave a romantic nationalist justification for the rejection of the international modern style were what distinguished German designs of the period (Figs. 47 and 48).

Italian partnerships

Modern Italian national design traditions are associated with style, flamboyance and provocative ideas, and arise primarily from the years after 1945. Italy gained a similar prominence to that of Scandinavian countries for its design, but for completely different reasons. Late to industrialise and then with development at a very rapid pace and localised in northern cities such as Turin and Milan, traditional craft skills remained intact in southern Italy. By 1952, however, an editorial in *Domus* magazine could declare: 'Italy has, with Piaggio's designers, characterised the scooter, and she has very well-designed motor-cycles like Motom "Delfino" and the Rumi; a great industrial motor-vehicle designer, Renzo Orlandi of Modena, and Viberti of Turin; the most attractive sewing machine in the world, the Visetta; Pavoni's espresso machine, Cassina's chairs and the Rima metal chairs and cabinets, the fantastic Pirelli floorings, Crippa's perfect packagings, and the "Carro di Fuoco", the Liquigas coach designed by Campo and Graffi: she has the two-deck OM railcars designed by Zavanella, the VIS writing desks by Rosselli, Albini's folding units for the Rinascente, the products designed by Zanuso for Prodest-Gomma, the Solari clocks and

46. A dining area in the hunting room of a house in Stuttgart, Germany, designed by Ernst Wolf, 1940, from *Das Schöne Heim* (House Beautiful), Munich, 1940

The design of this interior fulfilled 'völkisch' ideals of reviving regional traditions as advocated during the Third Reich. The wood panelling in larch, the lamp in wrought iron with pigskin shade, the craft patterns for the chairs, the linen textiles printed with hunting scenes and windows of antique glass were all testimony to local, handwork skills.

47 and 48. Paris Exposition Internationale Arts et Techniques dans la Vie Moderne, the German Pavilion by Albert Speer and the Pavilion of the Soviet Union by Iofan. Published by photo studio Kaczka et Besougly, Paris, 1937

The German and Soviet pavilions at the Paris international exhibition indicate that no clear-cut distinction can be drawn between architectural style and political ideology. The case might even be made that Neo-classicism became an international style, replacing Modernism of the 1920s and early 1930s.

watches by the Studio BBPR, the furniture designed by De Carli, Mollino, Romano and Vigano, the Arteluce lamps, etc. This means that the material is there, that there is an Italian bent for these things, and the beautiful, pure and simple "Italian line", without excessive burdens, has been finally recognised all the world over.'[59]

After the Second World War many Italians were uneasy about the legacy of architectural Modernism. Unlike Germany, Italy for a short period in the 1930s under Fascism had adopted modern design, which it called Rationalism, as its official style. Consequently, it has been suggested that Italian designers and architects were prepared to search for a revised modern language of design, no longer regarding the International Style as experimental or avant-garde, while other countries, such as West Germany and to some extent Britain, returned to the first principles of Modernism to invest them with a significance for their new situations.

One of the ways Italy cultivated its identity as the design centre of Europe was by means of the substantial government investment in a three-yearly furniture exhibition, the Milan Triennale (Fig. 49). Its themes in the post-war years indicate the move from necessity, to the aesthetic, and eventually to counter-cultural ideas of the mid-1960s. As Penny Sparke has commented, progressive design

34

U. R. S. S.
EDITIONS ART ET ARCHITECTURE

SECTION DE URSS

ARCHITECTE : IOFAN · COLLABORATEURS FRANÇAIS : BONNÈRES, COQUET, JOSSILEVITCH, ARCHITECTES

41

ALLEMAGNE ARCHITECTE : SPEEN · COLLABORATEURS FRANÇAIS : COURRÈGES, COUDERT,
ÉDITIONS ART JANKOWSKI, HUGONENQ, ARCHITECTES — EFFET DE NUIT
ET ARCHITECTURE

49. The Danish
contribution to the
Milan Triennale in *Domus*
magazine, Milan, November
1954, edited by Gio(vanni)
Ponti (Italian, 1905-1973)

In this page layout the
Italian and Scandinavian
approaches to design
converged with the
sculptural treatment of
chairs and bowls by Finn
Juhl, Kay Bojesen and
Herbert Krenchel.

ideas were pursued by major Italian industries.[60] This encouraged experiments with both traditional and new materials, especially plastics and foam rubber in furniture (Figs. 50 and 51). Crucially, design in Italy was considered a suitable medium not just for interpretations of good form but also for avant-garde ideas. The works were then discussed in the same journals as architecture, reflecting the architectural origins of many leading Italian designers.[61] This model of designing: aesthetic innovation; exhibition; high profile critical debate, became one that many around the world would aspire to in the years that followed.

50. Tea-table designed by Carlo Mollino (Italian, 1905-1973) and manufactured by Apelli & Varesio, Turin, taly, 1949. Plywood and glass with brass fittings. H. 51 1/2 L. 123 D. 54 cm W. 7 – 1985

The Italian government actively promoted design and industry after the Second World War. In addition to the three-yearly design exhibitions (Triennale) held in Milan, the Italian government sent a major travelling exhibition around the United States in 1950. The table was included in that exhibition entitled 'Italy at work: her Renaissance in Design Today'.

51. 'Dondolo' (Rocking Chair) designed by Cesare Leonardi (Italian, b. 1935) and Franca Stagi (Italian, b. 1937). Made by Elco, Venice, Italy, 1967. Moulded fibre glass. H. 85 D. 170 W. 39 cm. Circ. 329 – 1970

Moulded fibreglass is used to produce a single looping form. The fluted moulding suggests movement while providing a high ratio of strength to weight. Although apparently never mass-produced, it was featured in the firm's showrooms and at the annual Milan furniture fair.

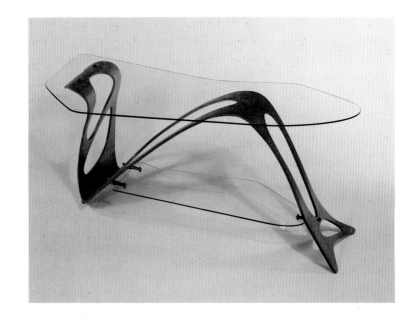

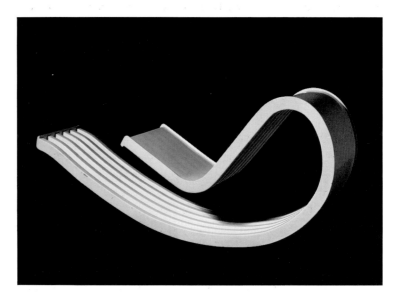

'In 1972 a major exhibition of Italian design was held at the Museum of Modern Art, New York, entitled "The New Domestic Landscape". In addition to the inclusion of many "classic" designs from the previous decade, it also featured a number of interior environments created both by leading protagonists of mainstream Italian modern design movement – Joe Colombo and Gae Aulenti – and by a number of designers associated with the anti-design movement – Ettore Sottsass, Superstudio and Archizoom. The aim of the latter was to 'recontextualise' the object and to provide 'microenvironments' which encouraged new ways of sitting, eating and relaxing, rather than perpetuating object fetishism.'[62]

In 1981, the Memphis design group was formed in Milan under the direction of Ettore Sottsass (b.1917).[63] Sottsass had already acted as design consultant for Olivetti and Poltronova before working more experimentally in Studio Alchymia. He gathered around him a group of young Italian and international figures who had a common interest in subverting hierarchies of 'high' and 'mass' culture. Part of their strategy was to move beyond the maxim 'functional necessity' in design, by working on its emotional and sensorial levels. They did this by playing with the conventional meaning of materials, structure and colours. They also mixed languages of popular culture with architectural references in small domestic items (Figs. 52 and 53). More than any other design group, Memphis signalled how design could operate simultanaeously on both a national and an international level, as a set of objects which comprise a 'look' or 'style', and also as a serious attempt to reinvest material culture with deeper meaning, as a critical language. The objects were not originally intended for everyday consumption, although their potential for mass production was always encouraged. Since the publication of its avant-garde manifestos, in fact, many of the stylistic attributes of Memphis designs have been translated into new styles for popular goods.

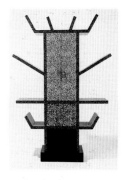

52. 'Casablanca' sideboard by Ettore Sottsass (Italian, b. 1917), and made by Memphis, Italy, 1981. Plastic laminate over fibreboard. H. 228.6 W. 161.3 D 39.4 cm W. 14 – 1990

The Memphis tradition encouraged designers to employ brightly coloured patterned surfaces (in this case: red, yellow, black and greys) and to explore the possibilities of plastic laminates. An 'Italian' approach broke rules, challenged assumptions and incorporated humour.

'Englishness'

'Naturalness makes up the best part of the Englishman's character. And we see this character in its present-day form reflected in the English house more truly and clearly, perhaps, than in any other manifestation of English culture.' Hermann Muthesius (1861-1927).[64]

To a commentator in this century, the term 'English house' may evoke a more modest type of dwelling than the English country-house of

53. 'La Conica' Expresso coffee-maker, designed by Aldo Rossi (Italian, b. 1931), 1982. Made by Alessi SpA, Milan, Italy, 1984. Stainless steel and copper. H. 29.5 W. 13.5 cm M. 5 – 1990

Rossi is one of several internationally acclaimed designers to work for Alessi. His designs apply architectural metaphors to domestic objects. His famous 'Teatro del Mondo' for the Venice Biennale was a floating structure moored in the Lagoon. It was one of the first explorations of the cone and tower, reworked in this coffee-maker.

previous centuries. Nonetheless, it has played a crucial part in defining what for many is regarded as the national character of 'Englishness'.

Such is the complexity of 'national character' that Muthesius's original study of the English house took three volumes. He concentrated on a tradition which was common to the south of England. By contrast, an account of the other parts of Britain including the 'Celtic Fringe' would have introduced other associations, especially concerning the craft values of materials and vernacular patterns. As Muthesius commented, the English house encapsulated attitudes to private and public space formed by social, religious and political customs as well as tastes imposed by climate and geography. His subheadings give an indication of his interesting approach: 'Individuality of the English a result of the country being an island'; 'Living in private houses'; and 'Ethic significance of the fireplace'. *The English House* was extremely important for European readers in its recognition and definition of Arts and Crafts ideals and the near-contemporary aims of the Garden City movement.[65]

Muthesius examined the dictum 'truth to materials', one of the longest-serving legacies of the twentieth century from the design reformers. This was also identified by John Gloag, in 1946, as a part of *The English Tradition in Design*.[66] The belief was that to reveal construction in woodworking, leaving surfaces unadorned, or to use decorative devices which enhanced natural features were more 'honest' ways of working (Fig. 54).

In 1956, the architectural historian Nikolaus Pevsner continued the debate on English national style when he published *The Englishness of English Art*.[67] With the proviso that national character does not at all times and in all situations appear equally distinct, Pevsner went on to describe what he suggested might be called a 'geography of art'. Attributes of 'Englishness' from town planning to painting included conservatism, reasonableness and good sense, a pursuit of nature and respect for the picturesque traditions derived from the English Romantic movement (Figs. 55 and 56).

Pevsner wrote at a time of reconstruction in Europe. His foreign eye allowed him to notice the distinctive nuances of modernity. A

54. Table, designed by
C.F.A. Voysey (British,
1857-1941) in 1903,
made by F. C. Nielsen of
London, 1905-6. Oak
H. 75.5 W. 68.5 cm
W. 19 – 1981

This table demonstrates
Voysey's concern for truth
to materials. He specified
'no nails or screws' were to
be used in the construction,
and the wood was meant
to be left unpolished and
unstained. This maxim
was embraced by many
British designers and
furniture makers in the
twentieth century.

critical reader might be encouraged to think of exceptions to
Pevsner's account. What of Britain as workshop of the world, as the
first industrialising country and a nation of inventors and scientists
with implications of progress?[68] Or indeed, could Britain be a nation
of commercial entrepreneurs unrestrained in matters of style and taste?

A student of Pevsner, Peter Reyner Banham, posited *The New
Brutalism* as an alternative approach identifiable among those
working in Britain in architecture and design.[69] Alison and Peter
Smithson, members of this generation, qualified the change in
sensibility: 'Gropius wrote a book on grain silos, Le Corbusier one
on aeroplanes, and Charlotte Perriand brought a new object to the
office every morning; but we collect ads...Mass production
advertising is establishing our whole pattern of life – principles,

55. Bowl: 'Boat Race', Designed by Eric William Ravilious, (British, 1903-1942) Made by Josiah Wedgwood and Sons, Etruria, Staffordshire, 1938 Earthenware, transfer printed W. 31.7 x H. 14 cm Circ. 379 – 1939

The simple form and glaze of the bowl is in the spirit of Wedgwood's 'Queensware' introduced in 1765 and the technique by which the decoration is applied relies on the continuing tradition of transfer-printed engraving. Even the subject-matter of its decoration, the boat race first rowed between crews from Britain's oldest universities in 1829, has a national significance.

56. Two- and three-storey housing designed by Robert Shepherd in Harlow New Town and featured in the magazine *Architectural Review* in 1955

Originally designed for a population of 2,000, Harlow was considered 'perhaps the most successful work of "townscape planning"' at the time in Britain. Forest-size trees were incorporated in the plan with additional planting of indigenous trees. The mixed development of houses and flats owed much to European and especially Swedish precedents.

morals, aims, aspirations and standard of living. We must somehow get the measure of this intervention if we are to match its powerful and exciting impulse with our own.'[70]

In the larger parallel phenomenom of Pop design more significance was given to graphic design, fashion and furniture, often seen as experimental and expendable ways to re-define the environment. In Britain this might be regarded as a valid reaction to the high seriousness of Modernism and the historicism apparent in other parts of the design tradition. In many respects Pop was vernacular in its stress on locality: the city, the town and the street (Fig. 57).[71] It encouraged visual and verbal puns, a quick-wittedness in playing associatively with language. Above all, it was defiantly commercial, rejecting distinctions between high and low culture, which had so often been inherent in much earlier design writing.

The significance of the retail-led movement in design was noticed by a later commentator on British (now no longer separable as 'English') identity. Frederike Huygen wrote when the impact of privatisation on many of the former nationalised industries and services was manifest in corporate identity schemes and new marketing strategies in Britain. Accordingly she attributed a national identity which arose from a pioneering, style-led service economy at the expense of product innovation and design (Fig. 58).[72]

57. Page layout from the magazine *Nova*, London, April 1967 with photographs by Harri Peccinotti

This magazine was central to the promotion of Carnaby Street and the Pop phenomenon in London. The article captured the mix of graphic style and decoration, applied to the human body, clothes and shopfronts and interiors, so much a hallmark at the time.

58. Midland Bank, Britain designed by Fitch RS, Rodney Fitch (British, b. 1938)

In Britain the most extensive re-design of a major banking group was carried out for Midland Bank by Fitch RS in 1986. Following market analysis and customer research the design identity separated three functions into different spatial areas; immediate services (money transmissions), speedy services (enquiries), and expert advice (customer interviews).

59. Poster advertising 'Benetton' clothing, c.1989 'United Colors of Benetton', Luciano Benetton (Italian, b.1933), photographer, Oliviero Toscani (Italian, b.1942) Printed in Italy by Elli Pagani

This advertising campaign used the apparent internationalism of modern photography, akin to 'The Family of Man' which was the title given to a photographic exhibition in 1955 by Edward Steichen. It implies that Benetton unifies people around the world in terms of colour, creed and nation.

60. Page spread from iD magazine, London, March 1993

The London-based style magazine ran a competition to customise the Sony Walkman. The winners in this case were two London streetwear designers, Mau Mau and Insane. They represent how an internationally familiar product can acquire regional identity.

Regionalism and Globalism

'It is most interesting to compare the many museum catalogues of "well-designed objects". Whether printed in the twenties, thirties, fifties or seventies, the objects are usually the same: a few chairs, some automobiles, cutlery, lamps, ashtrays, and maybe a photograph of the ever-present DC-3 aeroplane. Innovation of new objects seems to go more and more towards the development of tawdry junk for the annual Christmas market, the invention of toys for adults. When plugging in the first electric toasters in the twenties, few would have foreseen that in another brief fifty years the same technology that put man on the moon would give us an electric moustache brush, a battery-pack-powered carving for the roast, and electronic, programmed dildos.'[73]

Ethical questions raised by Victor Papanek in his book *Design for the Real World* in 1971 recalled the critique of industrial production formulated by others a century earlier. Morris had written in 1885: 'For all our crowded towns and bewildering factories are simply the outcome of the profit system. Capitalistic manufacture, capitalistic land-owning, and capitalistic exchange force men into big cities in order to manipulate them in the interests of capital; the same tyranny contracts the due space of the factory so much that (for instance) the interior of a great weaving-shed is almost as ridiculous a spectacle as it is a horrible one. There is no other necessity for all this, save the necessity of grinding profits out of men's lives, and of producing cheap goods for the use (and subjection) of the slaves who grind.'[74]

As we know, Morris could not reconcile his ideals of craft production with the need for goods affordable by the greater proportion of the population. Those cheap goods and their proliferation are a concern for many involved in design issues today. They still raise insoluble questions of the division of labour, de-skilling and poverty of materials. For instance, to keep costs of production as low as possible, many industrial goods are increasingly the result of part-work of a cross-global kind. The

61. Point of sale material for 'Ecollection' by ESPRIT Clothing, San Francisco, USA, 1993

ESPRIT clothing responded to the growing awareness of ecological concerns in the fashion industry by taking control of the entire textile cycle. This involves growing cotton free from pesticides on land owned and cultivated by the company, paying fair wages and supporting rural workers, incorporating safe techniques for colours with no bleaching and using recycled paper for packaging.

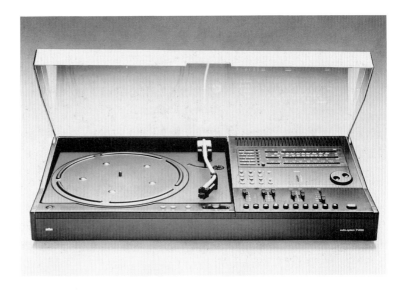

62. Audio System P 4000, 1973 designed by Dieter Rams (German, b.1932) and manufactured by Braun Product Design, Braun AG, Kronberg, Germany

Each of the components of this system, record player, cassette deck and receiver amplifier, can be built into the cabinet singly or in any desired combination. The formal sophistication of Rams' designs have become a standard by which the functionalist and minimalist approach to product design could be tested as an accepted international idiom.

toxic effects of many man-made fibres are now known and the dangers of certain production processes take designers back to natural materials (Fig. 61). Increasingly the criticism is not just those of design theorists, but of consumers of design, who want to know more about the implications of the processes used for their goods. Ethical consumerism is an equally international phenomenon and exerts considerable influence.

Interestingly, commentaries on late-industrial society have turned attention from the productive forces to systems of communication and consumption in a technologically sophisticated world. The Canadian sociologist and communications expert, Marshall McLuhan (b.1911), argued that the mass media of television, radio, newspapers, books, records and tapes provide rapid global dissemination of information, linking countries which share this experience as if in a 'global village'.[75] McLuhan suggested that such experience is 'cold' or intrinsically poorer than live experience. Whether or not they agree with this diagnosis, designers now have to work with the tools of this technologically developed society.

Postmodern commentaries since McLuhan have argued about the philosophical and moral implications of a world in which cultural difference is vulnerable, with the reduction of spatial distance

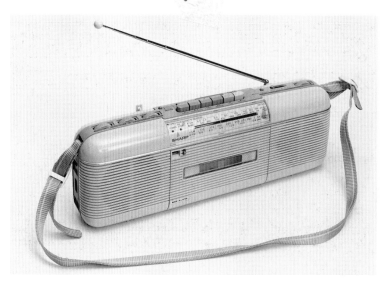

63. Sharp Portable Stereo Radio and Cassette Player, Model QT 50 E (P). Designed and made by Sharp Corporation, Japan, 1986. Polystyrene case and synthetic fabric strap. W. 13 – 1992

Sharp's QT 'retro' style coloured radios, such as this pastel pink version, were inspired by models of the 1940s and 1950s. They contrasted with the many chrome and matt black models then available. Although originally designed for the Japanese youth market their popularity abroad prompted other manufacturers to reconsider their approach.

through air travel and temporal distance through broadcasting by satellite.[76] It is now likely that urban populations around the world share more attitudes and common life expectations with one another than they do with rural populations in their own countries. Manufactured and designed goods contribute significantly towards this apparent commonality of urban experience, from Buenos Aires to Bangkok. Objects used in the home as equipment and as luxuries may be stratified globally (or horizontally) rather than by nation (or vertically). A roll-call of international company names equips these efficiently-heated homes with televisual entertainments, computers and electronic goods which in turn contribute cycles of fashion, style and music (Fig. 59).[77]

As histories of design testify, no sooner has a level of similarity or homogenisation occurred globally then regional inflections appear: 'customised' mass-produced goods. The status of the object in this form of consumption is therefore a curious blend of global similarity and regional difference (Fig. 60).

What are the possibilities for design in such a world? Certain objects, it would seem, continue to move towards the elimination of any cultural and social inflection which might indicate a country of origin or associative meaning. Increasingly, multi-national companies

64. Gimson single ladderback chair designed by Ernest Gimson (British, 1864-1919), made by Neville Neal (British, b. c.1920), Stocton, Warwickshire, 1971. Ash frame with rush seat. H. 105.4 W. 39.4 x D. 47 cm Circ. 119 – 1971

Gimson's ladderback is based on a seventeenth-century pattern. Neal was an apprentice of Edward Gardiner (d.1958), the first craftsman to make Gimson's version of this chair. Still made today, the chair represents an unbroken tradition, not a revival.

require products which are compatible with many diverse contexts; their unobtrusiveness should denote efficiency, but allow other more personal aspects in the lives of their users to dominate. Dieter Rams (b.1932), head of the design division at Braun electrical goods, has formulated a list of ground-rules for design (Fig. 62):

'Simple is better than complicated
order is better than confusion
quiet is better than loud
unobtrusive is better than exciting
small is better than large
plain is better than coloured
harmony is better than divergency
being well balanced is better than exalted
continuity is better than change
sparse is better than profuse
neutral is better than aggressive
obvious is better than searching for things
less elements is better than many
system is better than single elements.'[78]

Electronic industries have adopted a black aesthetic for hi-fi and televisual apparatuses for many years. Although the wish to be culturally non-specific is a useful marketing strategy, a commentator on design should recognise that this attitude, like all others, is determined and comes from a design tradition. In his early career Rams worked with Hans Gugelot (1920-1965), who had taught at the Ulm Hochschule für Gestaltung, an important research-based institute concerned from 1955 to 1968 to explore systems design. Historians will argue whether there is perhaps something inherently 'German' about this serious approach in its acceptance of standardisation and a search for a functional aesthetic. One way to solve this would be to consider a range of electrical companies, German and non-German, and contrast their approach to product semantics (Fig. 63).[79] An added paradox is that Braun is no longer German-owned. What in fact constitutes the national character: attributes in the objects, organisation of the company, or the intellectual traditions of education which inform such design?

65. The 'Europa' table
designed by Nigel Coates
(British, b. 1949),
manufactured by Bigelli
Marmi, Italy, 1992.
L. 200cm W. 140cm H. 75cm

To mark the entry of the
United Kingdom into
Europe, Coates' design
incorporated the figure of
Europa carried by Zeus in
the form of a bull with a
border of the twelve stars
of the European parliament.
The combination of mixed
materials and narrative
decoration is characteristic
of a postmodern approach.

Rams's list implies that there is a single meaning to design, concerned to find an ultimate quality. In many circles it is now agreed that meaning in design is a cultural construct, reinforced by stereotypes and ideas in visual and verbal language. In the face of such cultural relativism, interest in handmade and craft traditions has grown significantly. To many people their values appear longer standing and less susceptible to the vagaries of fashion which an urban situation introduces. In the twentieth century, we have to be careful in assuming that this is so; many folk or rural 'traditions' are in fact the result of more recent revivals or inventions (Fig. 64).[80]

One important strand within Postmodernism has been a move to insert a regional dimension into design. A persuasive argument for this was presented by Kenneth Frampton in an architectural essay 'Towards a Critical Regionalism'.[81] Frampton's is a useful concept to apply to many of the strategies of designer–makers in recent years, both in their ideas for marketing and production. Regionalism can involve insensitive appropriations of local style, but the 'critical' approach Frampton advocates needs an intelligent reworking rather than straightforward revivalism. Frampton suggested that regionalism need not be retrogressive; instead, architects and designers might consider ways in which local character can be incorporated in their choice of material, symbolism and acknowledgement of context.

66. 'Consumer Rest' and 'Short Rest', prototypes of chairs, 1983 by Stiletto Studios, Berlin. Manufactured by Brüder Siegel, Germany, 1990

By using the supermarket trolley in their designs for chairs, Stiletto Studios highlighted the conventional distinctions between commercial and domestic spheres. The titles played semantically with the associations of such source materials.

New legislation for European countries in 1992 and moves to abolish internal national barriers encouraging free transfer of goods, services, people and capital in a single market provided a new context for design. Alongside this, historical identities in regional areas have been re-forming in political or cultural ways, as in Austria and Hungary or Catalonia. In 1991 an exhibition shown in Paris and Düsseldorf under the title 'New European Design' predicted the opportunities that this might encourage (Figs. 65 and 66). In a group drawn from what might have been exclusively the capital cities of Europe, there were instead representations from Barcelona, capital of Catalonia but not Spain; Milan, traditional furniture capital of Italy; Düsseldorf, Cologne and Berlin, all significant cultural cities in Germany, but not the seat of government at the time.[82] The tendency of the designs on display was towards the polemical. Ideas and materials challenged conventions. Designs were produced in small-scale workshops and intended for galleries, a version of a 'Sezession' or withdrawal from the orthodox context of large-scale fairs and mainstream imperatives. We might conclude that design responds in more flexible ways to its economic base than simply in terms of 'nation' and its geography will become more fluid. Aided by new technologies it will readily take on new versions of cultural and ethnic identity to meet the diversity of markets in a worldwide context.

Notes

Publications which appear in the Further Reading List at the end of this book are given by author and date in the notes; all other references are complete in the notes.

1 For Germany see B. Hinz, *Art in the Third Reich*, Blackwell, Oxford 1980; for Italy see *L'Anni Trenta, Arte e Cultura in Italia*, Comune di Milano, Mazzotta, Milano 1982. As yet, there is no study of design under Stalinism in the English language, but see A. Tarkhanov and S. Kavtaradze, *Stalinist Architecture*, Laurence King, London 1991.

2 J. Meier Graefe, 'Wohin treiben wir?', in *Dekorative Kunst*, cited in Troy (1991), p.31

3 First distinguished by Louis Coujarod in 1892.

4 The Enlightenment is the term used to characterise the philosophical and humanistic traditions which proposed the progress of humankind through the development of rational and scientific thought. These emerged in Europe and North America in the late eighteenth century. The late twentieth century has witnessed a questioning of the fundamental principles of the Enlightenment.

5 J. Bentham, *An Introduction to the Principles of Morals and Legislation*, T. Payne and Son, London 1789.

6 *The Electrician*, 578/2, 29 September 1883. For an account of electrification see Thomas P. Hughes, *Networks of Power, Electrification in Western Society 1880-1930*, The John Hopkins University Press, Baltimore and London 1983.

7 For the context of typographic change in publishing, see L. Febvre and H. J. Martin, *The Coming of the Book*, NLB, London 1976. A good starting point for consideration of the national schools of typography is the writings of Stanley Morison, see, for example, *Selected Essays on the History of Letterforms in Manuscript* 2 vols. Cambridge University Press, Cambridge 1973.

8 See R. Kinross, *Modern Typography, an Essay in Critical History*, Hyphen Press, London 1992, p.145.

9 A useful corrective to the idea that visual language can ever be universal is offered in the article by E. Lupton, 'Reading Isotype' in *Design Issues*, vol.iii, no.2, Chicago, also published in the anthology ed. V. Margolin (1989).

10 For a review of German poster design which is especially strong in this kind of approach, see the catalogue *Kunst! Kommerz! Visionen! Deutsche Plakate 1888-1933*, Deutsches Historisches Museum, Berlin 1992. For a history of the poster see D. Ades and M. Friedman, *The 20th Century poster: Design of the Avant-garde*, Walker Art Center, Abbeville Press, New York 1984.

11 Antoni Gramsci, *Selections from the Prison Notebooks*, Lawrence and Wishart, London 1971. On artistic autonomy and the politics of culture, see J. Wolff, *The Social Production of Art*, Methuen, London 1981.

12 On the situation in the Indian subcontinent, for instance, see H. Kumar Vuyas, 'The Designer and the Socio-Technology of Small Production', in *Journal of Design History*, vol.4 no.3, Oxford 1991.

13 C. Wilk, *Thonet: 150 Years of Furniture*, Barron's, Woodbury, New York 1980.

14 The definitive account of the Bauhaus is provided in H. Wingler (1978) and an interesting reassessment is in G. Naylor (1985). The Bauhaus Archiv, Berlin has been most prominent in research and exhibitions, see *Bauhausarchiv Sammlungskatalog*, Berlin 1981. The Dessau Bauhaus also has archives and an exhibition programme.

15 For consideration of the Bauhaus as a commercial venture, see A. Rowland, 'Business Management at the Weimar Bauhaus', in *Journal of Design History*, vol.1 nos.3-4, Oxford 1988.

16 Quoted in Banham (1960). *Buckminster Fuller*, Trefoil, London 1990, p.180 suggests that this criticism was written twenty-eight years later than Banham initially indicated.

17 J. Joedicke, *Weissenhof Siedlung*, K. Krämer, Stuttgart 1989, English and German text.

18 W. Lotz, 'Suites of Furniture and Standard Furniture Designs', originally in *Die Form*, vol.11, pp 161-69, Berlin 1927, translated and reprinted in *Form and Function*, eds. C. Benton, T. Benton and D. Sharp, Open University Press, Milton Keynes 1975.

19 After the essay by the German philosopher Immanuel Kant (1724-1804), 'Critique of Aesthetic Judgement'. See also, M. Podro, *The Critical Historians of Art*, Yale University Press, New Haven 1982.

20 Le Corbusier, *Towards a New Architecture*, Architectural Press, London 1970, first published as *Vers une architecture*, Editions Crès, Paris 1923. Also see the journal edited by Le Corbusier and A. Ozenfant, *L'Esprit Nouveau*, Paris 1920-25.

21 See Museum of Modern Art catalogues, *The Machine Age*, New York 1934 and *Bauhaus 1919-1928*, New York 1938, reprinted 1975.

22 H. R. Hitchcock and P. Johnson, *The International Style*, W. W. Norton, New York 1932, reprinted 1966.

23 For a fiftieth anniversary reappraisal of this exhibition see T. Riley and S. Perrella, *The International Style*, Rizzoli, New York 1992.

24 Franz Kafka, *America*, (1927) Penguin Books, Harmondsworth 1967, p.46.

25 S. Giedion (1969).

26 See for example, D. Hounshell (1984), D. Noble, *America by Design: Science, Technology and the Rise of Corporate Capitalism*, A. Knopf, New York 1977, and A. Pulos, *American Design Ethic*, MIT Press, Cambridge, Mass. 1983.

27 A. Pulos, op. cit. p 85.

28 See D. Hounshell (1984), Chapter 6, 'The Ford Motor Company and the Rise of Mass Production in America'.

29 For example, see evidence of this in P. Maguire, 'Designs on Reconstruction: British Business, Market Structures and the Role of Design in the Post-War Recovery', in *Journal of Design History,* vol.4 no.1, Oxford 1991.

30 In R. Loewy, *Industrial Design*, Faber and Faber, Boston and London 1979; also see Loewy's earlier autobiography, *Never Leave Well Enough Alone*, Simon and Schuster, New York 1951 and A. Schoenberger, *Raymond Loewy, Pioneer of American Industrial Design*, Prestel Verlag, Munich 1990.

31 'Plastics in 1940' in *Fortune* magazine, vol. 22, October 1940. For a consideration of the meaning of plastics, see J. Meikle, 'Into the Fourth Kingdom: Representations of Plastic Materials 1920-1950', in *Journal of Design History*, vol.5 no.3, Oxford 1992.

32 Quoted in E. Hobsbawm (1990), p.5, footnote 11.

33 Other forms of classification available to the art and design historian are outlined respectively in M. Pointon, *History of Art*, Allen and Unwin, London and Boston 1986, J. A. Walker, *Design History and History of Design*, Pluto Press, London 1989, and H. Conway, ed. *Design History: a Student's Handbook*, Allen and Unwin, London 1987.

34 Extremely vibrant adaptations of Futurism were made in Soviet ceramics, see N. Lobanov-Rostovksy, *Revolutionary Ceramics: Soviet Porcelain 1917-1927*, Studio Vista, London 1990, and for Czech Cubism see A. von Wegesack (1992).

35 A. Forty (1986).

36 Barthes' essay on Panzani foods is 'The Rhetoric of the Image' in ed. S. Heath, *Image Music Text*, Collins, Glasgow 1979; see also R. Barthes, *Mythologies*, Paladin, St Albans 1973.

37 K. Nishihara, *Japanese Houses – Patterns for Living*, Japan Publications, Inc.,Tokyo 1968.

38 See E. J. Hobsbawm (1969) and J. Joll (1976).

39 On the international exhibitions see P. Greenhalgh, *Ephemeral Vistas: Expositions Universelles, Great Exhibitions and World's Fairs, 1851-1939*, Manchester University Press, Manchester 1988.

40 N. Pevsner, *Academies of Art Past and Present*, Cambridge University Press, London 1940. See also the article, A. Coombes, 'Museums and the Formation of National and Cultural Identities' in the *Oxford Art Journal*, II,ii, 1988.

41 C. R. Ashbee, *An Endeavour Towards the Teaching of John Ruskin and William Morris*, The Essex House Press, for E. Arnold, London 1901. For a compilation of Morris's writings, see ed. A. Briggs, *William Morris: News from Nowhere and Selected Writings and Designs*, Penguin Books, Harmondsworth 1984.

42 For a case-study of Morris's impact on Hungary see K. Keserü, 'The Workshops of Gödöllö: Transformations of a Morrisian Theme', in *Journal of Design History*, vol.1 no.1, Oxford 1988.

43 W. Gropius, *The New Architecture*, Faber and Faber, London 1935, p.42.

44 J. Campbell, (1978) and L. Burckhardt *The Werkbund*, Design Council, London 1988.

45 J. Heskett, *Industrial Design*, Thames and Hudson, London 1980, pp.88-89.

46 N. Pevsner, *Studies in Art, Design and Architecture*, Thames and Hudson, London 1968; section XIII 'Patient Progress Three: The DIA'. Also F. McCarthy, *A History of British Design 1830-1970*, Allen and Unwin, London 1979.

47 N. Troy (1991), pp 52-103.

48 ibid p.58.

49 ibid p.79, originally published as 'L'Art Décoratif au Salon d'Automne', in *Gil Blas*, 2, 12 October 1911.

50 W. J. Schweiger, *Wiener Werkstätte: Design in Vienna 1903-1932*, Thames and Hudson, London 1984.

51 A useful account of the tensions in this British movement is given in J. Woodham, *The Industrial Designer and the Public*, Pembridge, London 1983.

52 G. Selle, *Die Geschichte des Design in Deutschland von 1870 bis Heute*, DuMont, Cologne 1978 and H. Oehlke, 'Design in der DDR', in *Vom Bauhaus bis Bitterfeld*, ed. R. Halter, Anabas Verlag, Giessen 1991.

53 Stockholm, Nordiska Museet, *Model Sweden – An Exhibition of Modern Sweden*, 1987, D. McFadden (1982) and catalogue Victoria and Albert Museum (1989).

54 Review of the Paris Exposition Universelle, in *The Studio*, London 1901, pp.221-3.

55 Quoted in Segerstad (1961), p.14.

56 A. Saint, *Towards A Social Architecture: the Role of School Building in Postwar England*, Yale University Press, New Haven and London 1987.

57 In German language see S. Günther, *Design der Macht – Möbel für Repräsenten des 'Dritten Reiches'*, Stuttgart 1992. In English, a preliminary study of the framework of National Socialist legislation is provided in J. Heskett, 'Modernism and Archaism in the Third Reich' (1980) which was re-published in B. Taylor and W. van der Will, *The Nazification of Art: Art, Design, Music, Architecture and Film in the Third Reich*, Winchester Press, Winchester 1990.

58 The official journal for art and design was *Die Kunst im Dritten Reich*, Munich 1937-39, which then became *Die Kunst im Deutschen Reich*, Munich 1939-44. It included reports on crafts and the decorative arts as well as painting and sculpture.

59 Quoted in A. Branzi and M. De Lucchi, *Il Design Italiano degli Anni '50*, RDE, Milan 1985, p.27. For an outline of the shifts in Italian design see V. Gregotti 'Italian Design 1945-1971' in E. Ambasz (1983).

60 P. Sparke, '"A Home for Everybody?": Design, Ideology and the Culture of the Home in Italy, 1945-1972', in P. Greenhalgh (1990).

61 For example, *Domus*, Milan, 1928 –.

62 P. Sparke, op. cit. p.200.

63 B. Radice, *Memphis*, Thames and Hudson, London 1985.

64 H. Muthesius, *The English House*, eds. D. Sharp and J. Posener, Crosby Lockwood Staples, London 1979, originally published as *Das Englische Haus*, Wasmuth, Berlin 1904 in 3 volumes.

65 On the Garden City Movement, see Ebenezer Howard, *Garden Cities of Tomorrow*, Faber and Faber, London 1946 and for a recent commentary on this and other ideas in town planning, see P. G. Hall, *Cities of Tomorrow: an Intellectual History of Urban Planning and Design in the Twentieth Century*, Blackwell, Oxford and New York 1988.

66 J. Gloag, *The English Tradition in Design*, King Penguin, London 1946.

67 N. Pevsner, *The Englishness of English Art*, Penguin Books, Harmondsworth 1956, latest edition 1988. Also see H. Binyon, *Eric Ravilious – Memoirs of an Artist*, Lutterworth Press, Guildford and London 1983.

68 On the idea of Britain as an early and now declining industrial power see Michael Dintenfass, *The Decline of Industrial Britain*, Routledge, London 1992 and P. Wright, *On Living in an Old Country, The National Past in Contemporary Britain*, Verso, London 1985. For a discussion of the circumstances of British industrial manufacture in the nineteenth century, see R. Samuel, 'The Workshop of the World: Steam Power and Hand-technology in mid-Victorian Britain' in *History Workshop*, no.3, 1977.

69 P. R. Banham, *The New Brutalism: Ethic or Aesthetic*, The Architectural Press, London 1966.

70 A. and P. Smithson, 'But Today We Collect Ads', in *Ark*, Royal College of Art, London 1956, p.49, quoted in N. Whiteley, *Pop Design from Modernism to Mod*, Design Council, London 1987.

71 See N. Whiteley, 1987, op cit.

72 F. Huygen (1989).

73 V. Papanek, *Design for the Real World – Human Ecology and Social Change*, first edition, Granada, St Albans 1974, p.105.

74 'Useful Work and Useless Toil' in A. Briggs, 1984, op. cit.

75 M. McLuhan, *Understanding the Media: The Extensions of Man*, McGraw Hill, New York 1964 and M. McLuhan and Q. Fiore, *War and Peace in the Global Village*, McGraw Hill Book Co., New York and Toronto 1968.

76 A starting point for discussion of Postmodernism which considers architectural evidence as well the main philosophical ideas is D. Harvey, *The Condition of Postmodernity*, Blackwell, Oxford 1990.

77 H. Aldersey-Williams (1992).

78 F. Burkhardt and I. Franksen, *Dieter Rams Design*, Gerhardt Verlag, Berlin 1980-81 and Rams' own essay 'Omit the Unimportant', in *Design Discourse*, ed. V. Margolin (1989).

79 A. Morita, *Made in Japan: Akio Morita and Sony*, New York, 1986 and S. Bayley, *Sony Design*, Conran Foundation, London 1982.

80 E. Hobsbawm and T. Ranger, *The Invention of Tradition*, Cambridge University Press, Cambridge 1983. On craft revivals see P. Dormer, *Arts and Crafts to Avant-garde: Essays on the Crafts from 1880 to the Present*, South Bank Centre, London 1992.

81 K. Frampton, 'Towards a Critical Regionalism: Six Points for an Architecture of resistance', in ed. H. Foster, *The Anti-Aesthetic* (1983), republished as *Postmodern Culture*, Pluto Press, London 1984.

82 A. Branzi and L. Burckhardt (1991).

Further Reading

This is a list of titles suitable for additional study of the subject. General titles appear first including anthologies, thematic and survey texts, followed by books dealing with the traditions of individual countries.

Banham, Peter Reyner *Theory and Design in the First Machine Age*, Architectural Press, London 1960
A full and important study concerned with traditions omitted by Pevsner, including Italian Futurism and Expressionism. The author was also interested in developing Giedion's ideas on technology

Benton, C., Benton, T. and Sharp, D. *Form Follows Function*, Open University Press, Milton Keynes 1975
Useful anthology of critics', designers' and architects' writings from the period 1890–1939

Burkhardt, L., Branzi, A *Neues Europäisches Design*, Ernst and Sohn, Berlin 1991

Forty, A. *Objects of Desire – Design and Society 1750-1980*, Thames and Hudson, London 1986

Giedion, S. *Mechanization Takes Command: a contribution to anonymous design*, (1948) new ed. W. W. Norton, New York 1969
Influential book which considers design and mechanisation and offers social rather than formal reasons for its impact

Greenhalgh, P. *Modernism in Design*, Reaktion Books, London 1990
Useful recent collection of essays offering reconsiderations of many of the tenets of Modernism country by country

Harvey, D. *The Condition of Postmodernity*, Oxford University Press, Oxford 1991
Clear analysis of architectural and cultural Postmodernism and discussion of the economic and social intepretations of a 'Postmodern' era

Heskett, J. *Industrial Design*, Thames and Hudson, London 1980
Good, concise introduction to the subject with an emphasis on transport and interior design

Hiesinger, K. *Design since 1945*, Thames and Hudson, in association with Philadelphia Museum of Art, London 1983
Useful visual reference to the main figures in postwar design

Hitchcock, H. R. and Johnson, P. *The International Style*, (1932) reprint W.W.Norton, New York 1966
This book was published to coincide with an exhibition of the same title, and was the first application of the term 'International Style' to modern architectural design

Hobsbawm, E. J. *Industry and Empire*, the Pelican Economic History of Britain, vol.3 'From 1750 to the Present Day', Penguin Books, Harmondsworth 1969

Hobsbawm, E.J. *Nations and Nationalism since 1750 – Programme, Myth, Reality*, Cambridge University Press, Cambridge 1990
The author has contributed most significantly to rethinking the industrial revolution and its political consequences

Jencks, C. *The Language of Post-Modern Architecture*, Rizzoli, New York 1977
One of the first and most comprehensive collations of 'Post-modern' architecture seen as a stylistic rejection of the principles of Modernism. Jencks' categories can be tested against examples of design, especially his argument on the role of language in Postmodernism

Jervis, S. *The Penguin Dictionary of Design and Designers*, Penguin Books, Harmondsworth 1984

Joll, J. *Europe since 1870*, Penguin Books, Harmondsworth 1976
Still an essential text for those requiring an historical framework for design

Margolin, V. ed. *Design Discourse – History, Theory, Criticism*, University of Chicago Press, Chicago and London 1989
Anthology of articles originally published in the journal *Design Issues* (Chicago 1983) on the history and theory of design including an extremely useful chapter, 'Postwar Design Literature' by the book's editor

Pevsner, N. *Pioneers of Modern Design*, (1936) latest edition, Penguin Books, Harmondsworth 1988
First published as *Pioneers of the Modern Movement* in 1936, explaining the formal and stylistic understanding of modern design from Gothic Revival and Arts and Crafts in Britain and the Design Reform movement in Europe before 1914.

Sparke, P. *An Introduction to Design and Culture in the 20th Century*, Allen and Unwin, London 1982
Clear outline of the major tendencies in design, with a good range of examples and further reading

Aldersey-Williams, H. *World Design – Nationalism and Globalism in Design*, Rizzoli, New York 1992
Offers a model to approach the complex nature of global manufacture

Britain
Huygen, F. *British Design: Image and Identity*, Boymans Van Beuningen Museum, Rotterdam 1989
A Dutch museum curator's perspective on a national tradition, offered at a time when streetstyle was perceived as a particularly strong British phenomenom

Catalogue *Thirties – British Art and Design before the War*, Arts Council of Great Britain, London 1978
Excellent introduction to art and design of a decade with useful biographical profiles and a good bibliography

Jackson, L. *The New Look – Design in the Fifties*, Thames and Hudson, London 1991
Review of design in one decade, concentrating on official or approved taste

Pevsner, N. *The Englishness of English Art*, (1956) latest edition, Penguin Books, Harmondsworth 1988

ed. Sparke, P. *Did Britain Make It? Critical Issues in British Design of the last 40 Years*, Design Council, London 1986
Reconsideration of the first major British postwar design exhibition at the Victoria and Albert Museum, London

Czechoslovakia
von Wegesack, A. *Czech Cubism*, Vitra Design Museum and Laurence King, London 1992
Consideration of a much overlooked movement, which challenges many assumptions to do with style and nationality

France
Troy, N. *Modernism and the Decorative Arts in France: Art Nouveau to Le Corbusier*, Yale University Press, London 1991
Significant study on this important stage of French design

Arminjon, C. et al., *L'Art de Vivre: Decorative Arts and Design in France 1789-1989*, Thames and Hudson, London 1989
Concentrates on the French luxury traditions

Catalogue, *Design Français 1960-1990 Trois Déciennes*, C.C.I. Paris 1988
Provides English-language summaries by decade and some extremely useful visual references

Germany
Campbell, J. *The German Werkbund: the Politics of Reform in the Applied Arts*, Princeton University Press, Princeton, New Jersey 1978
Most thorough study of the influential design reform group

ed. Erlhoff, M. *Designed in Germany since 1949*, Prestel, Munich 1990

Heskett, J. *Design in Germany 1870-1918*, Trefoil Design Library, London 1986
Focusing on the early formation of a nation's significant design tradition

ed. Lindinger, H. *Ulm Design: the Morality of Objects, Hochschule für Gestaltung*, Ernst and Sohn, Berlin 1990

Naylor, G. *The Bauhaus Reassessed*, Herbert Press, St Neots 1985
A study which places the theories of Bauhaus staff in a wider design education context

Wingler, H. *The Bauhaus – Weimar, Dessau, Berlin, Chicago*, (1962) MIT Press, Cambridge, Mass., new ed. 1977
Most detailed study of the Bauhaus with a good bibliography

Japan
ed. Sparke, P. *Japanese Design*, Michael Joseph, London 1987

Italy
Ambasz, E. *Italy: the New Domestic Landscape – Achievements and Problems of Italian Design*, New York Graphic Society, Greenwich, Conn., Museum of Modern Art, New York 1973

Sparke, P. *Italian Design 1870 to the present,* Thames and Hudson, London 1988

The Netherlands
Troy, N. *The De Stijl Environment*, MIT Press, Cambridge, Mass. 1983

Staal, G. and Wolters, H. eds. *Holland in Vorm 1945 – 1987*, English version, *Design in the Netherlands 1945 – 1987*, Stichting Holland in Vorm, Gravenhage 1987

Catalogue *Design and Industry in the Netherlands 1850-1950*, Stedelijk Museum, Amsterdam 1986

Poland
Crowley, D. *National Style and Nation State Design in Poland from the Vernacular Revival to the International Style*, Manchester University Press, Manchester 1992

Scandinavia
Catalogue, *Scandinavian Ceramics and Glass in the Twentieth Century*, Victoria and Albert Museum, London 1989

McFadden, D. *Scandinavian Modern Design 1880-1980*, Cooper Hewitt Museum, New York 1982

Segerstad, Ulf Hård af *Scandinavian Design*, Otava Publishing Co, Helsinki 1961

Bernsen, Jens, Schenstrom, Susanne, *100 and 3 Great Danish Industrial Designs*, Danish Designrad, Copenhagen 1985

Soviet Union
Boym, C. *New Russian Design*, Rizzoli, New York 1992

Lodder, C. *Russian Constructivism*, Yale University Press, London 1984

Spain
Julier, G. *New Spanish Design*, Thames and Hudson, London 1991

The United States of America
Hounshell, D. *From American System to Mass Production, 1800-1932*, John Hopkins University Press, London and Baltimore 1984

Pulos, A. J. *American Design Ethic, A History of Industrial Design to 1940*, MIT Press, Cambridge, Mass.1983

Aldersey-Williams, H. *New American Design*, Rizzoli, New York 1988

Meikle J. *Twentieth Century Limited – Industrial Design in America*, Temple University Press, Philadelphia 1979

Index